SEAGULL MORNING

SEAGULL MORNING

The Cornwall of My Childhood

by

ELSIE BALME

TABB HOUSE

First published 1990

Tabb House, 7 Church Street, Padstow, Cornwall, PL28 8BG

Cover photography by Paul Spencer and Ray Bishop

Typeset by St. George Typesetting, Redruth, Cornwall
Printed by The Guernsey Press, Channel Isles

I would like to thank all those who have lent photographs for this book and in particular Mrs Rosa Thomas, Miss Phyllis Arthur, Mr Gerald Richards and Mr Kenneth Bawden.

Elsie Balme

LIST OF ILLUSTRATIONS

CONTENTS

CHAPTER 1

"Dear Jersey"

SEAGULLS! The sound of seagulls has been the background music to my life. Seagulls, lacerating the morning with their razor-sharp cries; decorating the day with their aerobatics; seagulls, riding out the evening tide with the setting sun turning their white throats to gold. Seagulls, even in the dark of the night sometimes, running in before a particularly bad storm. You would hear them crying, and pull the clothes further over your head, to shut out the weirdness and incongruity of their midnight wailings.

I was not born in Porthleven, though I cannot remember living anywhere else. We moved there when I was about eighteen months old, and since my father had been born and reared in the village, I was classified a 'Port'lev'ner' and gained entrée to the inner circle of village life. Not so my mother: it is hard in these times of mass invasion from 'up country' to realise that in the close little village society of pre-war days she had something of a rarity value, and whilst she was invariably treated with courtesy and respect, was nevertheless regarded as a member of an alien species. We were always amused by the tale of how, shortly after her marriage, two friends came to visit my mother from Scotland. My parents were then living on a rather remote

1

farm near Gunwalloe, and the visitors had to stop outside Helston to enquire the way.

"Edward Giles," murmured one old local. "Can't say I know 'un."

"'Ess you do," interjected his companion, "Why 'ee down to Little Nanspean."

"Aw," replied his friend, "you mean 'ee that married a *furriner*?" My mother, though she lived much of her early life in Scotland, and some of it in America, was in fact born in Kent, and spoke in restrained, elegant English.

It was in America that my mother met my father, who had gone there to work after the First World War and had stayed for about ten years. They returned to Cornwall and were married in Mawgan Parish Church, where a few years later I was christened. My father's farm was a small one; mixed, but with an emphasis on dairy cows. Amongst the herd was one cow, a Jersey, of which I was particularly fond. It was my habit to allow myself to be hoisted on to the back of this creature and taken for a ride round the farmyard, to which action the cow seemed to have no objection. On one occasion, when I was just over a year old, I was missed from the house and after much frantic searching my parents discovered me in the cowshed, embracing the back legs of the same cow and addressing her as "Dear Jersey". Although she was normally a fidgety beast and a notorious kicker, dear Jersey was standing absolutely motionless throughout the proceedings, an interesting illustration of the affinity which most animals seem to have with very small children.

I suppose if circumstances had permitted us to stay at the farm my childhood would have taken a rather different course from that which in fact it did. I would have grown up in a much more sheltered environment, in the quiet of deep countryside, surrounded by animals: Seraphina the sow (who incidentally once tried to bite off one of my feet), dear Jersey, and Bonzo the dog, who even in my infancy followed me wherever I went, and I would probably have had a horse of my own. I should have attended the tiny village school at Gunwalloe and all my friendships would have been with other country children from similar agricultural backgrounds. But it was not to be. The economic situation of the 1930s forced my father, like many others, to give up farming, and so it was that he returned across the Loe Bar to the village of his birth, that strange, grey, sprawling, rather ugly yet infinitely appealing village of Porthleven, with its rumbustious community life; its unabashed scandalmongering; its infinite capacity for interfering in people's private affairs; and its uncanny ability to draw back to itself those who belong to it, so that if you have lived there, then you will never be completely alive again anywhere else, because some part of you will live there for ever.

The first house in which we lived in Porthleven was in Gravesend, so called because of the numerous bodies of shipwrecked mariners reputed to have been buried in the cliffs there in bygone days. One local worthy, perturbed by the lack of Christian burial afforded to these unfortunates, erected a granite cross to their memory at the far side of Loe Bar, and then had to duplicate his effort by erecting another one on the cliff at Breageside to commemorate other sailors wrecked on that side of the village. The two sides, known as Breageside and Sithney Side, had at one time been separated by a tidal river and were named according to the parishes in which they then lay. Breageside has always had a fierce pride in itself, the reasons for which are not entirely evident to those who do not live there, since Breageside, to the untrained observer, has little to commend it. It faces due east, and is therefore cold in winter. By midday the sun has vanished from its lower reaches, which are overhung by a grim cliff, all of one hundred feet high. Its houses have no great architectural value. It has been suggested that the great

3

advantage of living in Breageside is that when you are there you cannot actually *see* Breageside, but command a magnificent view across the harbour to the rest of the village. Be that as it may, Breageside to this day retains its separate identity, to such an extent that its old nickname of Little Nation still sticks to it. The road there runs on two levels of the cliff, the upper or top road and the lower road, round the edge of the harbour. Between these two levels lie the remains of an ancient lime-kiln, at that time surrounded by a wasteland of fish stores, net lofts and garages with corrugated iron roofs.

For reasons best known to themselves, the Breagesiders long ago designated this astounding hotch-potch of untidy buildings an area of great natural beauty, and erected a wooden seat at the side of the top road, immediately above the lime-kiln. And a local wag wrote:

> Twinkle, twinkle, Little Nation
> Up above the Lime Kiln high.
> What a lofty situation
> You good people occupy . . .

Gravesend boasted no lime-kiln, though it had its share of net lofts, emitting delicious tarry smells when the process known as barking was going on. Barking was a process used for waterproofing nets and although the substance used for the purpose was not tar, it looked and smelled very similar to an uninitiated two-year-old. Tar! The black, glistening, bubbling fascination of tar! The big, beautiful blisters that popped up in the road on hot days, that you could burst with your feet if no one grown-up was looking your way. The rich, glorious stream of the stuff coming out of the boilers whilst half-naked men with sweat rivers on their grimed faces shovelled on the chippings! They might give you a few chippings to play with, if you went and talked to them during their dinner hour. Or the biggest and burliest of them might

4

swing you up in the air to peer in fascinated horror over the top of the tar barrel so that the fumes nearly choked you, and he would laugh and tell you it was good for your lungs. The modern child has no such pleasures. His roads roll, ready-made, out of a machine, and the joyfulness of tar is an alien experience to him.

But Gravesend bubbled happily with tar, one way or another, throughout most of the year. Our house there stood a mere fifteen to twenty yards from the top of the cliff. Like so many other cottages of its type, you opened the front door and walked straight into the living room. To your right was a wooden screen, which when you got round it turned out to be a bench, or settle, flanking a kitchen table. The window, at right-angles to the settle, had a window-seat in which no one ever sat. The strange thing was that this was so in every house. There was always a window-seat, and it was always full of red geraniums, a maidenhair fern, or last week's newspapers, or maybe even a birdcage, but there were never any cushions and you never sat in the window unless there was company to tea and you had to make extra room at the table.

The table itself, apart from mealtimes, modestly covered its nakedness with a chenille cloth, which made funny patterns on your elbows when you rested them on it to look at a book. The room was heated by a genuine Cornish slab stove – vintage Toy of Helston – black, with innumerable brass knobs in continual need of polishing. Cleaning the slab was usually done on Fridays and since it necessitated the use not only of gallons of Brasso, but also large quantities of black-lead, it was not surprising that Friday night was usually bath night in the village. There were few bathrooms in those days, certainly none in the cottages. Our lavatory was perched, alongside the one belonging to the house next door, on the edge of the cliff itself, and you had to cross the road to get there. This journey gave rise to the euphemism 'going across the road' when the calls of nature were to be answered. In the old days, the contents of the lavatories used to be emptied over the cliff at high tide, but fortunately more sanitary arrangements prevailed in our time, though many houses in the village still had no flush lavatories at the time of the 1939 war.

Also across the road was a building known as the loft. This was a small, rather dark carpenter's workshop, with a letter-box bearing the legend V R let into its outside wall, and a bench seat running round inside. On winter afternoons the old men of the locality would foregather in the loft, and chew tobacco and spit into the sawdust. All old men spat in those days, and no one really considered it indecent. Presumably it alleviated a good deal of chronic bronchitis. The old men wore a uniform. Seafarers all, they liked to advertise their calling with navy serge trousers, peaked caps, reefer coats and 'Guernsey frocks' – navy-blue sweaters upon the fronts of which the names of their erstwhile vessels were embroidered in semi-circles of white lettering about an inch high. Some of them hadn't sailed in those ships for thirty years – indeed, some of the ships were at the bottoms of oceans – but the legends on the old men's chests bore proud testimony to their one-time mastery of the seas. In the loft they talked of their sea-going days, but no one listened much to anyone else because each was only concerned with his own story, and occasionally they patted you on the head and called you ''my 'ansum'' as you played with the shavings.

Shavings are such useful things when you are two years old. If you hang them over your ears they become curls, bobbing long and golden and making you feel like the princess in the fairy story. If you hold one end and bounce them they make themselves into endless fascinating spirals. If you run with them they will fly out behind you in the wind. Throw them up in the air and they can be butterflies, or autumn leaves fluttering round your head. Sniff them and you can smell the great forests from whence they came, full of bears and wolves and other marvellous animals that you have only seen in picture books. The texture of them is exciting: curling them about your fingers you become acquainted with the joys of sculpture and endless delight of shapes.

On summer afternoons, when the old men had vacated the loft in favour of the harbour wall, I sometimes sat with my grandmother in the garden. It wasn't our garden; it was hardly a garden at all, measuring only about eight foot by six, with a low wall on the cliff edge bearing wild sea-pinks in season, and a narrow border filled with nasturtiums around the other three sides. No one, to my recollection, ever did any gardening there, but everyone, from time to time, took a chair and sat among the nasturtiums overlooking the sea when it sparkled blue on a fine day. My grandmother would sit there with her knitting – an endless collection of socks on which she always seemed to be turning the heel – and I would sit beside her on a stool, sometimes holding the ball of wool; sometimes pulling the heads off the nasturtiums and sucking the droplets of honey out of the bottom of the corolla; and sometimes watching, with a rather fascinated horror, the slow writhings of the fat, naked green looper caterpillars which proliferate among nasturtiums at certain times of the year. I was never able to like the caterpillars. There was a basic indecency about them, squirming about as they did with their soft bodies slithering and their spongy, sucking feet making lazy progress over the nasturtium leaves. Spiders one could understand. Even beetles. They had legs and they used them as I used mine. But the great, slow, clinging caterpillars – these were alien beasts and I detested them.

My grandmother was of great age and great proportions when I knew her. She was not tall and had probably been very dainty in youth, but the bearing and rearing of nine sons and a daughter had effected the usual considerable alterations in her shape. She was warm and sweet and cuddly but it was rather difficult to sit on her lap, partly

7

because her bulk left very little lap upon which to sit, and partly because, like so many old ladies of her generation, she dressed mainly in frocks of slippery black silk, reaching almost to the ankle. Sometimes the black was relieved by little flower patterns in white or mauve, and on chilly days she wore a shawl. By contrast, the dresses my mother wore were always in patterns of turquoise and white, or orange and yellow and brown, as summery as the afternoons. All the afternoons were summer in Gravesend. Winter was something which came in the nights, when the curtains were drawn and the oil lamp lit, and you sat by the fire in your dressing-gown after supper while your mother read aloud to you from Rupert Bear. Winter was when the wind whistled around the cottage, and the sea never stopped sucking at the cliffs, and the stones rattled up and down the beach below, and sometimes you would hear a seagull crying in the darkness.

CHAPTER 2

The Place and the People

WE spent two Christmases at Gravesend, but I can only properly remember the second one. The weather was very wild that winter, the sort of weather in which they say it is possible to lean over a cliff edge and be blown back again by the sheer force of the wind. I have never known anyone try this experiment, presumably for fear that the wind would change direction without abating in force, and blow its victim straight into the sea. Somewhere between the storms came Christmas, dark and cold but calm. We had a Christmas tree, squashed in from floor to ceiling in our tiny living room, and it had real candles on it. At tea-time on Christmas Day the candles were ceremoniously lit. Everyone, once in a lifetime, should see a Christmas tree with real candles; it is true they are dangerous, and frowned upon by the Home Safety authorities, but to sit in a darkening room at five o'clock on a December day, with the soft red glow from the fire on one side and the silvery glimmer of the Christmas tree bathed in gentle light from the tiny flames, on the other, is an experience which I would not have missed for all the electric fairy-lights in the world.

That Christmas was one of innumerable presents. I

9

received, among other things, no less than seven dolls, most of which I ignored completely, as I never cared much for dolls. There was one I rather liked, but unfortunately her sojourn was abruptly terminated when Audrey Laity, who lived just up the road, came in to view my presents and accidentally dropped an enormous glass paper-weight out of her pinafore pocket onto the poor thing's face.

It was about this time that Jossy came into my life. Jossy, viewed now from the safety and sentiment of maturity, was rather a nice doll. She was baby-shaped, with a washable rubber body, moveable limbs, and a solid, virtually unbreakable china head, fortified within by some heavy sort of packing made of straw and glue, which showed through in later years when her scalp became cracked. I regarded her with great suspicion. Her face was too human. There was expression in those eyes; character in that mouth. Jossy was obviously a force to be reckoned with. To make matters worse, my father, *my* father, who belonged to me and no one else, was disloyal enough actually to take a liking to Jossy. Picking her up in his big hands, he would bounce her on his knee, crooning softly "Dear Jossy, dear Jossy". The eyebrow he raised at my mother during these performances was lost on me, tense with repressed rage and misery, as this usurper of parental love was caressed, petted and spoiled. Her smug little doll face would watch me knowingly, arrogant in the security of favouritism. It was intolerable. I resolved to teach Jossy a lesson. It was my father who found her, stripped of the nice clothes my mother had knitted for her, upside down on the stone floor in the farthest corner of the scullery.

I do not think my parents knew whether to be amused or shocked at my vindictive jealousy; even so, they did not know of the brutal beating Jossy had received at my hands prior to her naked humiliation on the scullery floor. She was, ultimately, restored to a kind of favour. I kept her for years, and beat her sadistically and regularly because I had no brother or sister with whom to fight for my parents' attention.

If Jossy fulfilled my infant need of something to hate, then Teddykins fulfilled the corresponding urge to love. In this, too, I suppose I was no different from most other people. How many adult bedrooms, I wonder, are sanctuaries for large, bland-faced, well-worn and much-loved bears? How many grown men have blushed furiously when their mothers informed their fiancées "He still has his teddy-bear"? What strange hold has the bear over the human mind, that he can command such devotion, such respect, over such a span of time? At any rate, Teddykins came to stay, and he and I have never been parted for long. It was Mr Damon who brought him. The Damons, an elderly Scottish couple, lived rather stylishly in a fairly large house named Carn-del, on the cliffs on the Loe Bar Road. So far as Porthleven ever claimed to have any 'society' I suppose the Damons qualified as members. They employed what I believe used to be known as a cook-general. Her name was Mary, and she too was Scottish; as dour as Aberdeen in her manner, but with a kindly, generous heart for all that. Both my parents worked for the Damons from time to time. My father looked after their garden and did other odd jobs; my mother occasionally helped in the house, and attended to those items of Mrs Damon's personal washing which were considered too precious to be committed to the dubious ministrations of the local laundry. Amongst these items were two satin blouses – one pink, one grey, with pin-tucked fronts and glass buttons. I coveted those blouses. I longed to deck myself in pink and grey satin, with glass buttons and pin-tucks. I watched my mother carefully laundering them; I listened to them squeaking when she wrung them out. They squeaked their way to a permanent place in my memory; I never see pink or grey satin, or pin-tucks, or glass buttons, without my mind reverting instantly to Mrs Damon's blouses.

11

The Damons occasionally gave small dinner parties for their little *elite* circle of friends, and my mother, dressed in a black silk dress and a white, lace-edged apron, would attend on these occasions to wait at table. On one unforgettable night, just after Christmas, I too went to the Damons' dinner party. Unable to obtain a baby-sitter, my mother had taken me with her to Carn-del – I remember it was one of the rare occasions when I actually rode in my despised and little-used push-chair – and I was deposited in the kitchen with Mary and told to be good. This was not difficult at first. A plate of cream-of-tomato soup kept me occupied for some time; I then turned my attention to Russian cream, topped with maraschino cherries. I heartily disliked the cherries, but the Russian cream was excellent. By the time the cheese and biscuits were being served, however, I was growing a little tired of eating. When Mary's back was turned, I sneaked out of the kitchen and followed my mother, at a safe distance, to the dining-room door. Through the crack I could see Mrs Damon, resplendent in oyster *crêpe de chine* and pearls.

Somewhere out of sight there would be other ladies in pretty frocks. I badly wanted to see, but I had been forbidden to go in. Perhaps, if I just peeped round the door . . .

A retired brigadier-general was the guest of honour at the dinner party and as the guest of honour he must not be gainsaid. He liked little girls, and he had had rather a lot to drink. He was in jovial mood. The party retired to the drawing-room, where he and Mr Damon became horses, first an obligingly slow and steady pair of old shires, crawling about on all fours over the carpet – then a couple of spirited Arabs, neighing realistically and rearing on their (ever so slightly unsteady) hind legs, with one delighted small girl rider basking in the focus of their attention.

There was a sequel to this episode. A few days later, out walking with my mother on one of the rare dry afternoons that winter, I espied my friend the brigadier also taking advantage of the better weather to enjoy a stroll. Not one whit abashed, I detached myself from my mother and joined him, seizing his hand delightedly. To my mother's intense embarrassment, he insisted on accompanying us for the rest of the walk. Although I have since been escorted by members of all the armed services on different occasions, I have never again held hands with a brigadier.

My father worked at this time in a local garage, owned and run by a family named Wills, and known colloquially as Willziz. Willziz, situated on the square in the middle of the village, was to all intents and purposes a profitable concern, though it never looked profitable – perhaps this was a matter of policy. You entered past an assortment of aged petrol pumps, and overhead innumerable metal advertising signs rattled and creaked ominously on rusty-looking brackets. Beyond the dark green front door you groped your way through a narrow covered alleyway filled with drums of various motor oils, metal jugs for decanting these, and bits of marine engines. To the right was what passed for an office, filled with boxes of sparking plugs, sets of spanners in dirty cloth bags, and ancient bills and receipts on spikes.

The whole place reeked of petrol and oil, and at the back where the repairs were carried out the floor was treacherously soft with deposits of the sticky oil and dirt mingling together like some disgusting sort of carpet.

The establishment was presided over by Johnny Wills, who dressed like a squire or a gentleman farmer in tweed plus-fours and check socks, and was rather frightening because he never seemed aware that you were there, so that you formed a vague suspicion that he might at any moment tread on you like a beetle, because he hadn't seen you. His son, Courtenay, was a much less fearsome person, who dressed in the proper garage man's uniform of an oily boiler suit, and occasionally spoke to you. He once even gave me a doll which he had won at a whist drive. She was made of celluloid in an alarming shade of mulberry red, and was dressed entirely in beads and coloured feathers. I named her Jemima, and found her rather amusing.

One of Courtenay's duties was the charging of accumulators. Wireless sets were highly popular in the village at this time, but few were connected to mains electricity, and carrying the accumulator down to be charged was a normal chore in most households. There were two places where you could take it: Willziz on the one hand, or Mr Needham on the other.

Mr Needham charged accumulators in a room at the back of the largest local grocery shop, an establishment known as Blight's. I mourn the passing of Blight's. It was such a reassuring sort of place. Like Willziz, it had its own very definite smell – a smell of bacon and cheese and dried fruit. The bacon hung, neatly covered in muslins, on enormous hooks from the ceiling, and grown-up people had to dodge between the sides of bacon as they made their way to the counter. The cheese, in vast slabs, reposed on a corner of the counter itself. Gilbert Blight was something of a connoisseur of cheese, and ate enormous quantities of it daily. It was a secret dream of mine to go round the counter and cut off half a pound of cheese with a wire. One day Blight let me try, and to my chagrin I found I could not get the wire through the cheese. Beside the cheese stood an enormous block of lard, and Blight could cut an accurate half a pound with one sweep of his enormous knife. The dried fruit was kept in drawers under the counter, and was dipped up with a scoop into thick little paper bags – blue for currants, brown for sultanas. Behind the counter were masses of little drawers. These contained spices and herbs, and if one of them happened to be open when you went into the shop the whole delicious aroma was rendered even more delightful.

While Mr Needham charged accumulators in the back

shop, his brother-in-law Gilbert Blight, an enormous man, served at the counter and commented upon the news. He was persistently rude about Methodists, Socialists and Women, all of whom he effected to despise, yet he seldom lost a customer. Perhaps this was because most people knew, although he did not mention the matter publicly, of the scores of bills which from time to time he wrote off because those who had incurred them were unable to pay. Neither did he refuse to serve them when they came back for more. I have a theory that his philanthropy embarrassed him and that he insulted people in order to give them an excuse not to be grateful.

Blight was in every sense of the word a character, in a community which abounded in characters. Two who impinged very much on my early consciousness were a couple of old men known as the Twinnies. Their real name was Mitchell, and for variety they were sometimes called the Twinnie Mitchells. Identical twin bachelors, they had retired from farming together some years before I was born and lived in a house in Wellington Road. Rumour had it that one of them had once been issued with a paternity summons, whereupon both had turned up in court, and the unfortunate complainant had been unable to identify her man.

But I could not appreciate such nuances when I first became acquainted with the Twinnies. They were the first identical twins I had ever seen, and they fascinated me for this reason. They had red faces with identical walrus moustaches and identical benign expressions. They dressed identically, usually in rather thick tweed suits, raincoats, bowler hats and black boots, the latter very highly polished. Sometimes they wore identical flowers in their buttonholes, and always they sat in identical pose, side by side on the windowsill of the chemist's shop on the square, watching the world go by. Occasionally, if you spoke to them nicely, they would refute their reputation for meanness and give you a halfpenny or a penny.

15

It is amazing to remember just what could be obtained for such a small sum of money then. The decision of how to spend a halfpenny could be quite an agonising matter. You could have an ice-cream from an establishment in Fore Street, known as None-Go-By, the chief distinguishing feature of which was an entrance gate which creaked rustily every time it was opened. None-Go-By sold two flavours of ice-cream, strawberry and vanilla, both equally delectable, and the choice was thereby rendered that much more difficult. However, although I liked ice-cream, I loathed having to eat the biscuit in which it was contained, and was therefore more prone to spend my money on liquorice bootlace, rolled up round a coloured sweet, or a lollipop, red, yellow or green from Mrs Sluman's shop in Gravesend or Mrs Kitchen's in The Gue. I remember once having a lengthy and earnest conversation with a small friend on the exciting possibility of blue lollipops, and how splendid life would be if they were obtainable.

Near the top of Fore Street, just down the road from Wimbleton's butcher's shop and across the road from chapel, stood another pair of grocery shops. A pair is the only phrase suitable to describe them, for although they purported to be business rivals, they were in fact a pair in almost every sense of the word, and almost as identical as the Twinnies. Each had a small window, which was stuffed to capacity with packets of soap powder, drums of salt and cardboard cut-outs of the Bisto kids. Each had a solid-looking counter inside, running the length of the extremely small premises, with a pair of old-fashioned scales with brass weights. Each had a wooden bench against the wall opposite the counter, on which you could sit while you waited your turn, and a chair beside the counter, where you could sit whilst actually being served. In both the shops, jars of jam, tins of beans and a few other commodities were stacked on shelves behind the bench, and those waiting there would help out by turning round and handing across the various items as they were required. In both shops, too, tins of biscuits were piled up from floor level in front of the counter, and if you wanted biscuits you had to find the right tin and hand it up. Each of these emporiums, which sold everything from clothes-pegs to black treacle, was kept by a spinster lady, Addie in the one instance and Gladys in the other. Addie's and Gladys's shops were a way of life. Just as the old men might gather in carpenters' or shoemakers' shops, or blacksmiths', so the womenfolk would assemble in Addie's and Gladys's to hear the news and chat about the burning topics of the hour while they waited to be served. If you were in Addie's shop and she did not have a particular product, she would send you next door to see if Gladys had it, and vice versa. It was an odd arrangement, but it seemed to work well. The exteriors of these remarkable premises were treated as one; indeed, they formed one building, the upper storey of which was heavily decorated with enormous metal advertisements for such products as Brasso, Brooke-Bond tea and Feathery Flake flour. No doubt the modern planners would regard it as a mess, but it was a colourful and interesting mess.

One of the reasons I so greatly enjoyed shopping in my early years was that it meant I could be with my mother, rather than enduring the company of other children, with whom I tended at that time to be very ill at ease. I have never made friends particularly easily, and my early childhood friendships were extremely few. My first friend was a girl called Rosa, who lived next door to us in Gravesend. She was two years older than I was, but we had a great deal in common. Both rather imaginative, with a predilection for fairy stories, we spent a great deal of time together in a make-believe world, accompanied only by Teddykins and Mary Ann. Mary Ann was Rosa's rag doll – a battered and ancient creature of unenchanting visage – but to Rosa she was the epitome of beauty. A well-meaning relative once bought a replacement for Mary Ann, but the newcomer was rejected because ''She hasn't got a kind face''. From time to time Mary Ann would require a new nose, or mouth or the stitching on of an arm, or a new button eye. There was a considerable furore on one such occasion when my mother, having volunteered to sew a new eye on Mary Ann, found that I had swallowed the button intended for the purpose. I have often wondered what eventually became of Mary Ann. Perhaps two small sisters and the normal processes of growing up assisted Rosa to bid her a healthy good-bye. But one remembers her kind old face.

My other friend, Mabel, was the same age as me, but I did not meet her until we left Gravesend and went to live in The Gue. Mabel was born with a double portion of commonsense. She was practical and phlegmatic, and seldom lost her head over anything. She very quickly realised that one of her functions in life was to keep my feet firmly on the ground, and this she successfully accomplished over a long period of time, steering me through innumerable follies and emotional crises. I was always a great deal bigger than she was – and I fear gained a reputation over the years for being formidable – but this counted not at all with Mabel. She brooked no nonsense – and in fairness I must admit that her judgements were usually sound.

We moved to The Gue in the January before I was three years old. The gales which lashed the village all that winter reached their peak that month, and I still shiver at the recollection of trudging up and down Peverell Terrace between the two houses when my mother was cleaning and decorating the new house ready for occupation. The word new is not to be taken literally. Our new house was another elderly cottage, much afflicted, after the fashion of such buildings, with rising damp, but to me it was an exciting and thrilling experience. To begin with, we had our own furniture, the Gravesend house having been a furnished hiring. Cherished pictures appeared and were hung on the walls, and ornaments, mostly pairs of vases fashionable at the time, stood on the mantelpiece.

The cottage in The Gue represented to me the acme of refined living. To begin with, it had not only a kitchen, but a sitting-room, with a grate; something of which I had no previous recollection. Furthermore, housed in the sitting-room was that epitome of luxury, a three-piece suite. My mother heartily disliked that three-piece suite; it was too heavy; it was the wrong colour; she could not think why she tolerated it in the house. But the chairs were deep enough to hide in when you were three years old, and the sofa was big and bouncy; its fat, stuffed arms were wide enough to make horses when no one was looking, and sitting astride one of them you could ride over the hills and far away on a wet winter afternoon. A further refinement of life in The Gue was an indoor lavatory. Wonder of wonders, you did not have to go across the road any more. Above all, there was one's own bedroom, with pink-flowered wallpaper, and an enormous grown-up double bed, which served as an excellent trampoline upon which to bounce when my father had carried me upstairs on his shoulders at night.

There usually followed a ritual known as scruffing, during which I would be tickled till I shrieked for mercy, thrown up in the air and caught as I fell, and finally rolled up in the eiderdown, a helpless bundle, exhausted and giggling, and beseeching a story. My father, an excellent story-teller, was however also a terrible tease, and delighted in embroidering his deliciously anthropomorphic tales of woodland life by the inclusion of such details as the mesmerising of small birds by a cruel fox, and only the firm intervention of my mother would stop the narrative in time to save them from falling into his grinning jaws. By this time I was often in tears at the possible fate of the birds, and my father would be sent downstairs in disgrace, whilst my mother heard me say my prayers. These too were highly ritualistic, and included a lengthy list of aunts, uncles and

19

cousins upon whom the blessing and protection of the Almighty must be sought each night. We ended with the Lord's Prayer and then, if my behaviour during the day justified it, my mother would read me another bedtime story, this time of a sufficiently soothing nature to promote pleasant sensations during drowsiness, and to offset the inevitable tension which arose when, on being left alone to go to sleep, I observed that one of the shadows cast on the bedroom wall by the light from the landing bore an uncanny likeness to the head of a grinning, predatory fox.

The Gue gouged its way down what must at one time have been a cliffside, through a miscellany of buildings which for sheer variety must be unrivalled anywhere, even in other Cornish fishing villages, none of which is noted for its careful planning and layout. Here, smart stone-fronted villas jostled a granite works: the Christadelphian meeting room looked primly across the road at Mrs Kitchen's general store, where you could buy a pennyworth of broken biscuits for a dolls' tea-party; stables and garages and cottages (with and without front gardens) tumbled together in profusion down to the rear of the Methodist Sunday school, past Pearce's bakehouse and out into Fore Street at the far end. I was permitted from a very early age to go to Pearce's to fetch the bread, since it did not involve crossing the traffic line in Fore Street. The whole place smelled of yeast and saffron and currants and gingerbread. The gingerbreads were special biscuits known as parkins; they were thick, large, and rather soft, and were as unlike the brittle, hard, commercial ginger snaps one buys nowadays as good Cheddar cheese is unlike the soapy-tasting packages sold under that name in modern supermarkets.

Life in The Gue was hard for most people. Even in the villas a bathroom was a rare commodity, and the cottage dwellers were lucky if they possessed an indoor water-tap. We were among the lucky ones who did: though of course there was no hot water supply and like most others in the road, our back-kitchen contained a perpetually burning paraffin stove with a large kettle kept at the boil for cups of tea and subsequent dish-washing sessions. On Monday mornings my mother, like most of the other women in the road, would rise by six o'clock, remove the straw mats from the kitchen floor and fill the iron boiler – there was no copper or washhouse available, so the kitchen became a laundry room for the day. The boiler, containing the first load of whites, was set on the stove, while two baths, one for washing and the other for rinsing, were dragged from the back-kitchen and set up on two old chairs. Starch was made. The rinsing water would have Reckitts blue added for a fine finish to the whites. The mangle was screwed down. Buckets were set beneath it, to catch the drips. Breakfast came while the first boiling was still on the stove; lunch was prepared during the second boiling, and usually eaten after that boiling had been washed and hung out. Coloured articles, followed by father's heavy overalls, were washed after lunch. Then the baths were emptied for the last time – the sink being some twenty yards away across the cobbled courtyard, and shared with the occupant of another cottage – the kitchen was cleaned and the mats re-laid on the floor before tea. After tea my mother prepared to tackle a mountain of ironing.

The battle of wash-day was the climax of a difficult existence for housewives in The Gue at that time. Everything had to be done by cumbersome old-fashioned methods. Hot water for baths, for instance, was heated in the wash-boiler on the stove, and baths could only be taken late at night when all the doors could be locked. During the day it was hopeless even to close your door in The Gue. Doors did not count in that community. People popped in and out of one another's houses as of right. They gossiped, drank tea, borrowed a cup of sugar, and filled one another's net needles. Making nets was a major home industry. Everyone did it, even children, as soon as they were old enough to master the art. There were very few cottages you could enter without encountering a hook with broccoli nets or, during the war years, a camouflage net of vast proportions in process of manufacture, or some sprout nets being sewn up.

In my time you earned six shillings for sewing up a hundred sprout nets, and a really fast worker could manage to do a hundred a day. During school holidays Mabel and I used to do fifty each per week, working together in each other's houses. In term time we only managed twenty-five, but it was pocket money well earned and gave us an enormous feeling of independence.

When we were not busy earning our living, the children of The Gue made nuisances of themselves everywhere. It is impossible, in such small, close communities, for children ever not to be a nuisance. To begin with, there was always a good reason why we should not be where we were. Our day's activities might commence on the steps of the Christadelphian Hall – a favoured spot for playing hospitals, as each step could represent one bed and we could lay patients right up to the door. But the groans of the sick perturbed the neighbours, most of whom were elderly, and one of whom in particular would threaten to throw a bucket of water over us if we did not go away. Sometimes she suited the action to the threat, and we had to move in a great hurry to avoid a ducking. We usually did not move far.

The Christadelphian Hall was a wooden building, constructed at first-floor level across one of The Gue's many alley ways, thus making cunning use of space and disposing of the need for foundations or damp courses. The building was mounted on vast granite posts. The space beneath, known as 'up under' was an ideal place to play in wet weather. The ground there was always dry, but soft, so that you could draw circles for marbles or squares for hop-scotch, and the pillars made splendid divisions into houses or classrooms according to the game in hand. Unfortunately at the far end of up under there were more cottages, and more irate cottagers with buckets of water, so our sojourn there was usually brief, even in the wettest of weather.

Undaunted, we would progress royally down the road. Always there was a baby asleep, or an old person who was too ill to stand the noise, or a newly-painted gate or fence which it was feared we would damage, or danger from flying chippings if they were drilling the granite at Ching's. If someone was feeling particularly irritable, they might threaten to fetch the local policeman, a rather faceless individual named Scantlebury, who sounded, by reason of his name, much more ferocious than he actually was. I never recall that he actually received any complaints about our riotous behaviour in The Gue: the threat of him was usually sufficient to move us on. We usually ended up in Paddy's Yard. This delectable and utterly forbidden territory was owned, not by Paddy – indeed we had not then the slightest idea who Paddy might have been – but by a wrathful old gentleman named Austin Ruberry, who lived in Unity Road, an eminently respectable area of the village which was jeeringly referred to as Piano Street on account of the popularity of that instrument there.

Austin would make periodic visits to his yard, wherein lay a hotch-potch of ancient vehicles, loose tyres, pieces of wood, rusty kettles, broken barrels, crab pots, old boats, sheds, pits, heaps of sand and gravel and many other items to gladden the heart of a child. It was an adventure playground, ready-made – only we were not permitted to venture there. This, however, troubled us not one whit. We regarded ourselves as lords of Paddy's Yard, and considered that we were doing no harm to anything – indeed, for the most part we were not, since there were few items of any real value to be found in its precincts. So there we would gather, to loll in the long grass on a lazy summer afternoon, or to crack the ice in the puddles on a winter's morning

23

and to swarm like ants over the latest delightful piece of junk.

The element of danger only added to our pleasure; the cry of the lookout – ''under the punt'' – at the imminent arrival of Austin was perhaps the biggest thrill of the day. While he stumped about, checking locks and inspecting rubbish, we would crowd together under the punt, waiting with bated breath for Austin to go away and hoping that no mother would have the indecency to call one of us in for tea before he had gone. Sometimes we would be discovered and he would chase us out of the yard, arms flailing, using deplorable language and uttering grim threats whilst we, with all the natural cruelty of childhood, would laugh at how easily we could outdistance him.

Thus displaced from our promised land, however, there was nothing to do but begin the whole process over again and return, stealthily, to the Christadelphian steps, where with luck we might remain undisturbed till nightfall or hunger or inadmissible exhaustion drove us home.

The Gue contributed many characters to the village, some of whom, happily, are still alive. Amongst those who are not was a gentleman who rejoiced in the name of Mock Ivy. I believe his real surname was Laity, but it was, and indeed is, one of the peculiarities of Porthleven never to use a person's proper name if a suitable nickname could be found for him. In a fit of enthusiasm I once collected and began work cataloguing these nicknames, from as far back as the old men could remember down to the newest ones used by young boys of their contemporaries. I gathered several hundred, and sorted them out into an alphabetical list, (which is printed as an appendix at the back of this book). The more difficult task of finding the derivations of the names goes on more slowly. It is a fascinating business. Henry-Any-Colour for instance, acquired this astonishing appellation when he displayed a notice outside his premises 'Whitewashing done any colour after six o'clock.' Black Beetle was called after his fishing boat, a leaky old tub, which he used to tar thoroughly inside and out in a rather futile attempt to keep it waterproof. The boat's proper name was the *Morning Star*, but Black Beetle it was to all and sundry, and so was its owner.

However, I never was able to discover why Mock Ivy was Mock Ivy, although we never called him anything else. He was a strange, lonely man, living apart from his wife. The grown ups said that he drank too much; certainly he could regularly be seen in a highly inebriated condition on Saturday afternoons. It was whispered that he took methylated spirits in secret. He was very clever, and extremely fond of children. It was not unknown for him to give us sixpence to buy ourselves some sweets, and although we were rather afraid of him, with his ear-rings and his red-spotted neckerchief, we never refused his money. I cannot remember how he made that money, though he had a job to which he went most days.

At weekends when he was sober he would employ his time mending watches, at which he was extremely skilled, and rivalled the local jeweller, Mr Lobb. Maurice Lobb was another person who astonished you by making a living out of his business, which he conducted on the most unconventional lines. You would take him your watch, or your bracelet, or your earrings, and he would promise to mend them in a week. You never called back till at least a month had elapsed, because all Mr Lobb's weeks were at least a month long. Then he would regard you over the top of his half-moon glasses and say "Let me see my dear – I've had that little job rather a long time haven't I? Let's say sixpence, shall we?" And sixpence it would be. Maurice Lobb was a devoted Methodist: maybe divine providence looked after him, for he certainly did not look after himself.

Another great Gue character was Charlie Ching, who lived next door but one to us. Like Mock Ivy he lived alone, if alone can accurately describe a collection of pigeons, several cats and a dog. The dog, a greyhound, looked even more starved than greyhounds usually do, and was an inveterate dustbinner. It was, indeed, one of the few dogs in my life to which I could not take much of a liking, though I was sorry for it and occasionally carried some scraps round for it to eat. It was Charlie Ching who was responsible for one of my earliest Gue adventures. Waiting outside the house for my mother to go shopping one morning, I was espied by Charlie as he came shambling down the road. He asked me where I was going, and I told him. I then asked him where he was going, and was informed that he was heading for the blacksmith's shop.

Blacksmith's shops, like cobbler's and carpenter's shops, served at that time the double duty of old men's clubs. I had never been in a blacksmith's shop and the idea fascinated me. About ten minutes later, Mr Ching being a slow walker, we were ensconced on an ancient wooden bench near the fire at the smithy in Wellington Road, surrounded by bellows and horseshoes and sparks flying off the anvil. Sparks of a different kind flew when my mother arrived, having been directed by a co-operative public as to where I could be found. The unfortunate Mr Ching was upbraided relentlessly, and left in no uncertainty as to whether he should ever again conduct me to the blacksmith's shop. For me, worse was to follow. I was taken home, soundly spanked by my mother for running away, and reported to my father, who probably found the whole story funny, although at the time I was unaware of his amusement.

On one occasion my father spanked me himself – again it was for running away and scaring my mother out of her wits. This time, at the age of about four, I had given her the slip in the local recreation ground and come home alone through the village. I had a habit, in my early days, of wandering off in this fashion, without pausing to consider the consequences, either to myself or to anyone else, and my poor mother endured numerous panics, wondering whether I had got lost or been abducted, or fallen over the cliff or into the harbour. I never did fall into the harbour, though some of my contemporaries did. This was considered a great distinction, particularly if you managed to do it when the tide was out, and acquired concussion. The real honours, however, went to Phyllis Roberts, who fell in, bicycle and all, and emerged angry and bruised, but otherwise unscathed.

The old men were always saying that the harbour was not what it had been and would tell you about the days when they, as boys, had been able to walk across it at high tide on the decks of the many boats moored there. Denied this delight by a certain dearth of boats, we nevertheless found fascination in the harbour. For those who dared, there were enormous granite bollards to be leap-frogged, and punts, moored close in against the steps, to be borrowed without the consent of their owners and paddled around on the tranquil green waters. To descend those steps was something of a hazard, for they were green with algae and weed below high waterline, and terribly slippery to negotiate. At low tide, you could watch the birds making patterns with their feet in the mud. The whole area smelled of mud – sea mud – salty and oily and dirty and clean all at the same time. Mud and ropes and nets slung over horizontal poles to dry in the sun; nets and tarpaulins and pots and lines, all piled about – the tools of men's trade; the means of their livelihood, lying trustfully about the place like a mark of respect to the community's honesty.

The rise and fall of the tide; the putting to sea and the returning to port of the fishing boats; the tension when a vessel was late coming in, followed by the scenes of jubilation on the quayside when she finally nosed through the gapway, low in the water and heavy with fish; the rivalry for the position of top boat – such things were central to the life of the village, and punctuated the

27

sequence of our days. Every child was familiar with the numbers and names of the boats: *Snowdrop, Maid Marion, Endeavour, Energetic.* We each had our favourite boat, and supported them as vociferously as if they were football teams. Dipping seaward through the evening swell, they took on something of the nature of a civic procession, symbolising our community pride; the fierce independence of a people who live by the conquest of the elements. But men, even Porthleven men, are not always destined to be conquerors. One misty morning in June, the *Energetic* did not return. Cut down in the fog by a cargo-boat, she lay at the bottom of the sea, and all but one of her crew with her. They were brothers: five of them. The crying of the gulls that morning was a poignant lament for a desolated family and a shocked community.

In spite of such disasters, the fascination of the sea was unbroken, and on summer evenings young and old alike continued to foregather round the harbour. About once a month a steamer would come in, loaded with coal or cement or timber. On these occasions you would drop everything and rush down to the quay to watch the proceedings, though these, being dependent upon a high tide, were often somewhat slow to get started. Even after the pilot boat, PZ9, had put to sea there still seemed to be an eternity of waiting before the steamer actually approached the pierhead. The pier was and is a highly dangerous place: an inadequate rail runs along one edge; the other has always been totally unprotected, but nevertheless, provided your mother had forgotten to forbid it, you ran to the end in an effort to be among the first to spy the name of the ship. Many of these steamers were regular callers and some of the men had girl friends in the village, a practice much frowned upon by the more heavily respectable members of the community, but highly popular among certain sections of the young, if only as a source of the vicarious thrills of gossip.

The excitement as the steamer nosed through the gapway

would rise to a crescendo; pandemonium would break out. Men with fenders pushing boys back from the edge of the quay; dogs barking wildly; orders being given and countermanded; a great deal of swearing; children shouting and cheering; hooters blowing; water, swishing and rushing in wild torrents of foam at bow and stern; chains rattling. The seeming silence which followed would engulf not only the harbour but the entire village, as though the whole place, like the scarred and weatherbeaten old steamer, had cut out its engine and slid into a quiet berth.

CHAPTER 3

School

MY formal education began in September, 1938 when, at the age of four and a half, I was despatched to join the infants' class at what was then officially designated Porthleven Council School, later Porthleven County Primary School, but which was known by all and sundry as Board School. Porthleven boasted two schools – Board School being slightly larger than Church School – but there was little to choose between the two except in the matter of religious education. Church School pupils attended Church compulsorily once a week, and for their pains received a new shilling from the local squire every Christmas. Board School scholars had two days off for St Peterstide, the great Methodist festival held every year in June.

The pupils of Board School were of all ages from four to fourteen or even, in exceptional cases, fifteen. A fourteen-year-old boy can seem very large and frightening when you are a rather sheltered little girl of not yet five, and I was immensely relieved to discover that the infants shared a playground with the girls only. Even this was terrifying enough. Apart from Mabel and Rosa, and one or two other friends who came to tea from time to time,

I was acquainted with very few of the other children, and had not realised that there were so many in the world as seemed to appear in the playground that first morning. Furthermore, they all seemed to know exactly where to go and what to do, whereas I felt like nothing so much as a distressed calf, accidentally separated from its mother in Helston Market. I reacted much as the calf does, and bleated shamelessly for my mother who, rather to my astonishment, appeared to have abandoned me to the mercies of the mob, which latter was in fact much kindlier disposed than my fearful imagination had led me to suppose. Two older girls, Palma and Marjorie Goldsworthy, who lived near us and both of whom I admired intensely because of their extraordinarily long plaits, took me firmly into their charge and marched me between them into the school building, becoming my guides and mentors during those first nightmarish weeks, which seemed to me to pass in a blur of hysterical laughter and even more hysterical tears.

The many confusions of school were to me typified by the chaos in the lobby, as the school's apology for a cloakroom was always known. This gloomy apartment, approached through an echoing blue-flagstoned corridor, formed the core of the school building and was astonishingly ill-lit, mainly because the solitary window gave on to the blank end wall of Strike's net loft next door. Two grim and badly cracked washbasins were situated at the window end; the taps gave cold water only, when they could be persuaded to give any water at all, which was rarely, though oddly enough they often dripped, and long rusty channels scarred the ancient porcelain in consequence. The pegs on which we were supposed to hang our coats were much too high for infants to reach properly, and we therefore depended on the goodwill of senior pupils to perform this service for us. Further complication was caused by the fact that there were insufficient pegs to allow us to have one each, and you never knew whose coat would be flung over the top of yours. This worried me on two scores, firstly because one navy-blue mackintosh looks very much like another, and I was literally terrified of going home with the wrong one; secondly because I feared that a 'dirty person' (of whom there were a few, even though Porthleven has always enjoyed a reputation for cleanliness) might hang her coat over the top of mine, and that I might thus acquire, if not a deadly illness, at least a crop of fleas. It was by no means unheard-of to catch a flea at school in those days, and the fear remained constantly with me for a long time.

The infants' classroom was situated at the rear of the building. You could see the sky out of the windows, though they were placed so high in the wall as to prevent any other view from being obtained. Presumably this was deliberate policy on the part of those who designed the building around the turn of the century. I liked the classroom. It smelled, that first term, just as a room should smell on an autumn day – of old wood scrubbed clean, the desks polished, the air warm and slightly smoky. During certain prevailing winds in the winter it often became too smoky, as the teacher fought a losing battle with the Tortoise stove. These stoves, of which there was one in each classroom, were surrounded by brass-topped safety rails, and parties of senior girls were despatched round the school every Monday afternoon to clean the brasswork. The headmaster, whose name was Griffin, and who was usually known as Griff or Griffbo, was a great believer in pupil participation, and many years ahead of his time in this respect. Various senior boys, for instance, took great delight in spending a large part of the early morning going from class to class with lists, checking on the numbers of pupils who required milk, and collecting the money due for this luxury. They felt a sense of triumph in being excused arithmetic to perform this task, and seemed blissfully unaware that they were in fact beginning to learn to put arithmetic to its logical purpose. Another of Griff's schemes was to detail one senior pupil to take charge of one junior pupil whenever the school walked out in crocodile which, for various reasons, we did from time to time. To my disgust I was not allocated to either of my Goldsworthy friends, but put under the eagle eye of a tall blonde girl called Victoria, who for reasons not clear to me was nicknamed Tortoise. To do her justice, I always found Tortoise most friendly and helpful, and she certainly contrived most successfully to break the barrier of my excruciating shyness with strangers.

Our infant teacher was a rather stout spinster lady called Miss Mewten, whose white hair gave her a decidedly grandmotherly appearance, although she cannot at that time have been more than about forty-five years old. The impression of great age, however, served to increase one's confidence in her, and she was held in considerable esteem by most of her pupils, even though most of them persistently mispronounced her name, addressing her emphatically as Miss Mew*tun*, Miss Mew-*tan* or Miss Mew-*tin* when answering their names at roll call.

The timetable at Board School would be considered very dull by the standards of most modern schools, but it had one virtue highly important to young children – a safe, recognisable routine. Every day began with prayers – these involved the singing of a hymn, for which one of the teachers would accompany us on the piano, followed by a responsive service and an extempore prayer by Griff. Because he was a Methodist lay preacher he was accomplished in the art of extempore prayer; because he understood children, his prayers were relevant to their needs, and our morning devotions were, for this reason, usually reverent and meaningful. After prayers we dispersed to our own classrooms, where the first lesson was always scripture. In the infants' class, this often consisted of learning to recite portions of the Bible by heart. The chosen passages were mainly psalms, but as Christmas approached during my first term we learned 'And there were in the same country shepherds abiding in the fields' from Luke's gospel. I am still able to recite that passage from memory: furthermore I always feel a sneaking desire to recite it with the same sing-song intonation with which we repeated it day by day during these early weeks of school life.

Scripture was followed by arithmetic, as night follows day and for me with much the same effect. The darkening of my intellect at the mere mention of this subject was a tangible and dismal thing. Perhaps it was not so bad in the early days when one was permitted to count shells. The shells were so pretty, like little ivory carvings. They felt interesting when you rubbed them in your hands, and made enchanting patterns, so that you almost forgot the boredom of how many twos or threes made twelve as you grouped cosy little families of cowries on the desk before you. But later, when the shells had been outgrown, then arithmetic became a pain. 'If oranges are twopence halfpenny each, how many can you buy for one-and-threepence?' This type of question, often included in the 'Ten mental' which commenced arithmetic each morning, distressed and harassed me to such an extent that right up till the coming of decimal coinage I retained a horror of purchasing oranges priced in halfpence.

After arithmetic came break, which was welcome or not according to what game the bigger girls had decreed we should play. Sometimes the smaller children were left to their own devices, but on other occasions we were ordered to field for rounders, and having been born a butterfingers I dreaded this ordeal, as someone in the opposing team was sure to make a rounder whilst I fumbled the ball. Even worse were the days when it was decreed that we should play 'Woody Way'. This game, which seems to have gone out of favour in the present generation, was highly popular among the rougher spirits,

34

and depended for its success upon everyone joining in. It was basically a form of tag. One girl would be 'It' – in this instance the correct word was Woody. Standing alone in the centre of the playground she would shout "Woody woody way – if I can't catch 'ee today I'll catch 'ee tomorrow". Selecting a victim, she would chase her until she was caught. The two then held hands and chased a third girl, and so on until only one person was left running free. This person was Woody for the next game. It all sounds simple enough, but its element of danger and excitement derived from the fact that Woody, who always remained as a kind of hinge or swivel at one end of the chain, and as leader had complete control over the direction in which that chain would move, could by pulling hard enough cause it to swing violently across the sloping asphalt playground, so that the person at the other end, unless she was able to run extremely fast, would often be swung off her feet. Casualties during Woody Way were numerous, and ranged from cut knees and hands to minor concussion sustained when people were flung against the playground wall in the chaos. A rank coward, I was always secretly rather glad when something of this sort happened, not because I wanted the victim to suffer (although I was frequently the victim myself) but because an accident invariably put an end to Woody for the time being. Apparently things were even more violent in the boys' playground, and broken bones were not unknown as a result.

I did not shine at any playground games in my early days. Natural timidity caused me to fumble the ball, lose my balance, or commit some other childish atrocity, and I found myself the target of numerous jeers. Quite by accident, however, I discovered a means of redressing the balance. I had always been able, without any real effort on my own part, to walk on the tips of my toes like a ballet dancer, and I was found in such a position one day by one of the senior girls, a rather fierce tomboy named Jean, of whom I usually went in mortal fear. To my astonishment she was highly impressed at what she considered to be a great accomplishment and requested that I teach her to walk on her toes also. In a little while I found myself conducting regular toe-walking lessons for a number of pupils up and down the flat alleyway at the side of the school building. I dread to think what the local ballet-mistress, had there been one, would have said of my methods, but in the event the only complaints came from parents whose daughters were wearing out the toes of their shoes, and I was instructed by the school staff to cease 'teaching ballet' forthwith. But the lessons had served their purpose. I was no longer quite so afraid: I found that by trying I could catch a ball like anyone else: I could even keep my balance during a game of Woody Way – after all, was I not the only girl who could competently run about on her toes; did this not give me a superior sense of balance? Psychologically it worked well: the number of cut knees I sustained in the playground became decidedly fewer, and the quantity of my mortified tears decreased in a most encouraging fashion.

Break was followed by English lessons until lunchtime, and during our first term or so, this involved learning to write. There was no nonsense about children needing to experience learning through play or being unready to learn to write in those days. You had arrived at school: during the coming year you would have your fifth birthday and it was essential that before too much time had elapsed you should be able at least to write your own name and read simple sentences. Neither had the deplorable 'look and say' method then been invented: at least it had not reached Porthleven Board School. We learned the alphabet in cheerful, sensible fashion, chanting enthusiastically that A says Ah and B says Bu and scrawling rows of As and Bs with chalk on our writing boards as we did so. I had not been taught to read before coming to school, but it was no time at all before I and most of my contemporaries were able to write sufficient sentences to make 'compositions'. By this time, of course, we had graduated from chalks to pencils and paper, a promotion to which we did not in the least object, since it was much easier to keep one's hands clean when writing with a pencil. Ink was another story, and a great obstacle to be overcome. All the pens leaked and you got more ink on your fingers than on the paper – furthermore, this resulted in lack of concentration and the content of your work suffered in consequence. Worst of all, it was terribly easy to get ink on your clothes, resulting in unmovable stains which brought down the wrath, not only of teachers, but of parents, on your head. The compensation of the inkwell was that you could always fish in it with the pen nib when the teacher was talking, or writing on the blackboard, and horrid but fascinating lumps of thick sludge could be dredged up from the bottom.

Occasionally there was the ritual of cleaning the inkwells. This again was not entrusted to junior pupils, and was an exceedingly messy process which resulted, however, in sparkling clean white inkwells winking from the corners of the desks, and a fresh supply of ink, which was brought round in a large container by a senior boy and which gurgled out joyfully through a funnel into the wells. It occurred to me that it would be fun to have ink of one's own – ink in interesting colours, with which one could write exciting literature, rather than the dull blue-black decreed by the County Authorities for school exercises. I therefore spent quite a proportion of my small pocket money on bottles of ink – mainly purple and green, with which I wrote numerous poems and stories in my spare time, copying them painstakingly into exercise books to preserve for posterity. At school, members of the infants' class were not permitted to use full-size exercise books: instead, several books would be guillotined into halves across the middle, and these half-size books were allotted to us. My determination to have full-size books resulted in the expenditure of more pocket money, and my consumption of sweets at that time must have been exceedingly low.

The school did not have a tuck-shop in these days, but there was a small general store a few yards away from the main gates, where sweets, lollipops and fizzy drinks might be purchased in the lunch hour. The shop was kept by a gentleman named Watters, who was known colloquially as Jimmy Squat. Most of us were a little afraid of Jimmy Squat, a lean cadaverous man in his shop apron, but he stocked the most interesting and luridly-coloured sweets, and his fizzy drinks were splendid, though apt to make you sick if you drank them too fast.

At this stage in my life the worst part of my day was the journey home to lunch, because at this time I was totally without protection from the school bullies. In the mornings I contrived to avoid them on the road by getting to school early; but when we came out at twelve o'clock I was at their mercy. To do them justice, they usually did not hit you unless you first provoked them, which I never did, but their teasing and mockery could reduce you to a shivering jelly, while their total disrespect for personal property was alarming. You soon learned to abandon the practice of taking a ball to school to play with, for this would be seized with delight and hurled about the road, often ending up in someone's garden, and you would be too scared to go and ask for its return. If you wore a scarf, or gloves, or worst of all, a beret, these would as likely as not end up on top of a passing car amid hoots of merriment from your tormentors, chief amongst whom were Buster Williams from Gravesend Council houses, and Pat Russell, who lived at the top of The Gue, and from whom I was afforded some slight protection by friendship with his sister, but from whom I still shrank in terror for many years. After a while, however, I contrived to vary my route to avoid theirs, even though this meant going the long way round each lunchtime.

Afternoons at Board School proceeded at a much more leisurely pace than mornings, and on the whole were a great deal more varied, though they always included a period of what was known as group reading. Under this system, six or seven children would be seated together with copies of the same book, and would take turns to read paragraphs aloud to each other. The group would include one or two good readers, one or two average readers, and a couple who were slower. A leader was appointed by the teacher for the group, and if the slow readers had any trouble, it was the leader's job to help them with the pronunciation and understanding of difficult words. If the leader could not read a particular word or did not know the meaning of it, he or she would go to the teacher for guidance. The great advantage of the system was the amount of time it gave the teacher to spend with the really backward. Nevertheless, each group would receive a fair amount of attention from the teacher during the course of the week, and everyone was 'heard to read' at least a couple of times. The system worked well: the only time I remember it breaking down was one day when I had been appointed group leader, and another member of the group insisted on pronouncing the word wound (as in 'wounded soldier') to rhyme with found. By the time the teacher had arrived on the scene we had almost come to blows.

Once or twice a week we had various handicraft lessons. For juniors these usually fell on days when the seniors had departed to Helston to cookery and woodwork classes, which were available to them on specified days at the Grammar School. These days were very pleasant for us younger children: we had the playground to ourselves to enjoy games of our own choosing: the staff gave us their best attention, and there was often some interesting diversion planned to make the day more enjoyable. Handicraft classes, however, did not come into this category. For girls, these consisted mainly of weaving and knitting. It is hard, at this distance of time, to remember at which one was worst. Certainly I seldom completed a row of weaving correctly without having to pull it out at least once, and continually stabbed myself with the needle whilst sewing. I think, however, that knitting was the real '*bête noir*' for me. I had learned to knit before going to school, and in the relatively tranquil atmosphere of my home could manage to produce a tolerable scarf for one of my teddy-bears, or even, with assistance, a usable kettle-holder. School knitting was another matter. It had to be absolutely correct, and my habit of making stitches by splitting the wool was not tolerated; nor was the even more deplorable practice of dropping a stitch at the end of the row to make the number come right.

Knitting was compulsory, especially after the war had started. We had to knit long strips of edging for refugee blankets – interminable streaks of bilious green wool with which everyone but me seemed able to cope. We took them home with us at night, to finish the day's quota of rows. When Miss Mewten congratulated my mother on the great improvement in the standard of my knitting, my mother failed to inform her that much of this was due to the fact that after I had departed to bed each evening, she personally ripped out my regulation six rows and knitted them up again properly, lest I should be discouraged. It was many years before she confessed this guilty secret to me, and by then I could knit competently enough to be very grateful for the boost her deception had given my morale.

One of the very few acts of deliberate rebellion I remember in Board School stemmed from knitting. There were in a drawer in the large sewing cupboard a number of partly-knitted woollen vests. These, like the blankets, were destined to be given to refugees, about whom our staff seemed to have an obsession. The vests, which were not being knitted by anyone in particular, reposed in a drawer until such time as any competent female was short

40

of a job. This might be when the term's set piece of needlework had been completed – or at the end of a lesson when someone had a quarter of an hour to spare. Occasionally even one of the teachers would pluck out a vest and knit two-plain-two-purl furiously for ten minutes or so. Not unnaturally, the vests grew extremely grubby, changing their colour from pure white to a murky grey, their tension according to the individual who was knitting them at the time, and their shape accordingly. They were deplorable garments, and we shuddered to think of the plight of any poor soul who would actually wear them.

The crisis came one hot, thundery afternoon, when my friend Mabel and another girl, an evacuee named Pat Wogan, had misbehaved during sewing class. The teacher in charge, a fearsome lady named Miss Young, of whom most of us went in mortal dread, ordered them to put their sewing away and to take out two vests and knit them. The indignant pair marched to the drawer and proceeded with some defiance to pull all the vests off the needles and tangle the wool. It was a sacrificial act on their part: of necessity they were reported to Griff and severely punished – but significantly the vests were never again used as punishment work, even though, to our chagrin, they were restored by Miss Young and her minions to their respective sets of coloured bone needles and replaced in the drawer. I cannot remember the vests ever being completed: I suppose they were and that some unfortunate child somewhere was expected to wear them; yet there is a certain cupboard in Board School which I would not dare to open, even now, for fear that the vests, in all their horrid glory, might still be there.

One of the greatest treats afforded by the somewhat limited school space and curriculum were nature walks. These usually took us through Mill Lane, a thoroughfare now flanked by housing estates on either side, but then an unmade road, winding between hedges high enough to shelter us from the sea winds in the winter, spangled with primroses in spring and laden with honeysuckle in the summer. At the top of the lane we would have the Vicarage rookery pointed out to us: at the lower end the swamps and marshes of Dickie Wigs' Moors (now somehow transformed into a football field) offered a wealth of fascinating flora and fauna to delight the senses. Sluggish, muddy pools held innumerable tadpoles in season: minnows could be fished from certain well-concealed streams, where tasty watercress grew wild. The banks of those pools and streams were fringed with several varieties of rushes, and sheltered by tall withies, which the fishermen would occasionally come and harvest to make crab-pots. Flowers abounded; in particular the delicately lovely lady's smock, which carpeted the damp ground in the spring.

We loved these moors: when we were old enough we often went there to play after school on summer afternoons. We played at jumping rivers, and negotiating bogs, and usually went home with wet feet and dirty socks. In the shelter of the withies we sat and whispered secrets to one another, including vital information as to where babies came from and how they were made. Today's child discovers sex much as he discovers breakfast porridge, and he appears in consequence to place a porridge value upon it: we learned of it like a summer picnic amid the golden shimmer of the buttercups and the sweet, long grass, and thought of it in similar terms. It was not such a bad system.

At the side of Mill Lane opposite the moors was an old, rarely used barn, which belonged to a farmer named Ronnie Benney. This, too, was a source of delight in after-school hours, though some girls feared that the bats which hung in the beams would get into their hair. Bats or no bats, it was a delightful meeting place for gangs and secret societies, particularly in wet weather. When I was about ten years old, I was a member of a secret society which called itself The Robin Hood Club. Each of us took

42

the name of a character from the Robin Hood saga, and in Dickie Wigs moors and Ronnie Benney's barn we enacted the adventures of our hero. Unfortunately a certain enemy (designated the Sheriff of Nottingham, although in fact she was a rather undersized little girl) was lured to the barn on false pretences one afternoon and securely tied up, escaping only after a prolonged bout of hysterics and a considerable amount of fighting, during which heavy bruises and scratches were sustained all round. The victim's mother subsequently rampaged round the village, visiting the homes of all the miscreants and demanding that they be punished for the escapade. I had the fortune, or misfortune, to be left out of the whole affair, as I had been forced by my mother to visit an aunt that afternoon, and I never knew whether to be glad that I had escaped the general wrath and punishment which followed, or sorry that I had missed the most exciting adventure in the annals of the Robin Hood Club.

It was certainly not my normal practice to become involved in school vendettas, although my aloofness stemmed more from cowardice than from benevolence. It was not uncommon, in these matters, for a victim to find him or herself encircled on a street corner and beaten up quite severely by tormenting adversaries. I found myself dangerously close to this on one occasion, following an incident in a singing lesson. We had all been beating time with our feet, and since this accompaniment was not deemed to be either necessary or desirable, we were ordered to cease it forthwith. Several members of the class failed to obey the order and Griff, who was taking the lesson, required them to put up their hands and admit their guilt. A number of them did so, and were kept in after school as a punishment. One girl amongst their number (the same Jean whom I had taught to stand on her toes) was convinced that I was among the culprits and had not owned up. My assurances of innocence were of no avail: I was accused of being a liar, a cheat and a coward, and threatened with dire retribution for my imagined crimes. These threats continued throughout several days. Jean would hiss at me whilst distributing hymn books for morning prayers, advance on me threateningly in the playground, and then began systematically gathering together a punishment force from among her cronies. I lived in a reign of terror, sure that I should soon be beaten to death. I was saved by the fact that Jean quarrelled bitterly with her own sister, one Margaret, who was also made of very stern stuff. She too, had a band of supporters; they became my champions against Jean's forces, and by the time the family quarrel was repaired, the whole incident of the singing lesson had been long forgotten, and I suffered not a bruise.

Our singing lessons usually did not have such an inimicable outcome, and were popular occasions in the school day. Cornwall has a long tradition of fine singing, and Porthleven has always prided itself that it stands second to none in that tradition. Certainly I have yet to be in any place where a group of assorted voices, assembled together without practice and in many cases without technical knowledge of music at all, could break spontaneously into such tuneful harmonies of song as may be heard in any pub or any chapel in Porthleven, even nowadays. In what other place could a group of grammar schoolboys ever have been heard rendering negro spirituals in the bus shelter at eight thirty in the morning? What other workmen's bus, homeward bound from Culdrose Air Station at six in the evening, ever echoed daily to the strains of 'Guide me Oh Thou great Jehovah' with every passenger joining in with tuneful gusto? Where also, outside Italy, one summer after the war would it have been accepted as quite normal for Joey Allen to purchase a piano accordion and accompany himself on it in an unending song recital on the harbour head – in which singing he was often joined by whoever happened to be sitting about in the sun? Thus it was not unnatural that we children, with singing in our blood and our bones, should heartily enjoy our singing lessons. We were not greatly bothered with technical matters, though in the infants' class we sang 'Running up the scale we go and then run home to mother doh' as though it were another interesting song – and later on we tolerated and absorbed such mnemonics as 'Every good boy deserves fruit' and learned the differences between minims, crochets and quavers. But for the most part, singing lessons were for singing songs, and we were prepared to sing as long as the staff were prepared to let us sing. We sang of wise hermits who lived in woods, of old women who had their petticoats cut off up to the knees, and, inevitably, of Gossip Joan, My Dame's Lame Tame Crane and the disasters of the burning metropolis. Rounds were quite a favourite, in fact, partly because they injected an element of competition as to which group could keep going longest, but also as a means of demonstrating that we could sing in parts, and the ease with which most rounds were mastered was but another indication of the natural ability of a Porthlevener to sing.

During the war our repertoire became intensely patriotic, regularly including such gems of dubious musical merit as 'There'll always be an England' and the highly popular 'God Bless the Prince of Wales'. Since my mother had explained to me that we did not then in fact have a Prince of Wales I was a little bewildered as to why this particular song had to be sung so often, but it was frequently requested by someone who presumably either did not know or did not care about the monarchical structure at the time. We also sang 'Rule Britannia', which served double duty as a chorus for 'Three Old Bachelors' in the school playground. This game consisted of three people skipping round in a ring with chosen partners while we chanted:

Three Ole' Bachelors, all in a row.
Nothing to do and nowhere to go.
Choose to the east and choose to the west –
Choose to the one that you love best.

Rule, Britannia, Two tanners make a bob.
Three make eighteenpence
And Four, two bob.

At the conclusion of this performance the partners were supposed to kiss and part company, but since the game (in school hours, at any rate) was played entirely by girls, the kissing would be omitted. A variation of the song was sometimes introduced, which went

'Oyster Sir, an Oyster Sir,
An Oyster Sir,' she cry
'This is the finest Oyster, Sir
That ever you wish to buy.'

'Father was a fisherman
And that was all,' she cry.
'This is the finest Oyster, Sir
That ever you wish to buy.'

Where these songs came from, and how old they were, and how they came to be sung in the playground of Porthleven Board School, I do not know, but sung they frequently were, as was another, attached to a rather complicated game called 'The Big Ship Sails' in which everyone joined hands and performed a rather complicated dance movement until everybody's arms had got crossed over their fronts. I never fully determined the object of this game, but the song, which had a catchy tune, ran:

The Big Ship sails through the alley alley ay
The alley alley ay,
The alley alley ay.
The Big Ship sails through the alley alley ay
On the first day of November.

Or was it 'The *last* day of November?' Or was it

September, after all? Certainly we played it mostly in the late autumn, for the mere mention of it conjures up a picture in the mind of woollen jumpers, pleated kilts and knee-length socks.

On Friday mornings we had a special singing lesson devoted to the hymn-book. This came directly after prayers, and was a much awaited occasion, chiefly because it eroded so much arithmetic time that there was often no arithmetic at all, and certainly there would be no 'ten mental'. Griff, fully aware of our dubious motives, nevertheless indulged our requests for "just one more, sir," because, I suspect, he loved hearing children sing hymns. He was the Chapel choirmaster, and good hymn-singing was something of a passion with him. Besides the standard favourites, he taught us many new tunes which over the years became old favourites themselves.

At Christmas we sang ourselves hoarse. The Friday morning sing-song would continue till a very late break, and would often be resumed for an hour, by popular request, in the late afternoon. Sometimes the same carols were sung over and over again, especially the St Day Carol, which had then only recently been set down on paper, and of which, as Cornish children, we were naturally very proud. Also at Christmas we acted plays. They were very stylised nativity plays, and would probably make a modern drama teacher wince, but we enjoyed them, particularly when we took them on tour round the school. The reason for this touring was that the classrooms were small, too small to contain at once all the pupils of the entire school, a few of whom needed to take up half the floor space for use as a stage. So we would take our play round the other classes in turn, and there was a tremendous thrill in doing this. Mary, draped in a blue curtain, Joseph in folk weave bedspread, numerous angels in grubby white paper dresses trimmed in tinsel, with butter-muslin wings and head-dresses more

47

suited to Christmas tree fairies than celestial beings: a stiff-eyed, pink-faced doll, carefully bandaged, in a much too clean cradle – maybe they gave us a romanticised vision of Christmas, but I would not have had it any other way. There is time enough, when you are a little older, to contemplate the dirt and the squalor and the humiliation of the occasion – to argue the pros and cons of the Virgin Birth and suffer the endless dreary debates about the commercialisation of Christmas and whether or not the whole thing is a pagan festival christianised or a Christian festival paganised. Often, during such drab and colourless pontifications, I have wondered if the Almighty might not find a tinsel angel with starry eyes a more acceptable Christmas present than an earnest, utilitarian grown-up with neither mirth nor music in him.

Drama as such was not a subject included in the syllabus of Board School, but a teacher keen enough on the subject could weave it skilfully into other subjects and employ it as a useful teaching aid. In the Lower Junior class, we had a teacher whose great enthusiasm was acting: consequently everything was dramatised. We acted plays, poems, stories. History was acted. Scripture was acted. Even arithmetic was acted on occasions when the shop was brought out. This consisted of a vast collection of dummy packets of every conceivable product, including some mouth-watering bars of chocolate. During these shopping sessions we were not merely required to calculate the change correctly in the cardboard money provided, though this was the main object of the exercise, but we were also expected to think ourselves into the rôles of shopkeeper, housewife, or whatever we were supposed to be. We must make the right sort of over-the-counter conversation, behave politely to one another and attempt, in every way possible, to be grown-up. One's subsequent experience of the manners of many adults in shops leads one to wonder whether this, too, was not a rather romanticised view of life, but at least it helped us to know something of courteous behaviour.

For a little while, during this time, I rode the crest of a wave. Mental arithmetic apart, I found I could cope with most things, and was enjoying school at long last. I had a big part in a play. I began to feel successful. Then disaster struck. I was Put-into-the-Yellows, the most mortifying experience possible for any member of the lower junior class at that time. Board School did not boast a house system, but each class was sub-divided into four teams: reds, blues, greens, and yellows. This division was mainly for the purposes of games, when we wore hessian bands dyed in the colours of our team, and competition between us was fierce. In the lower junior class, however, a system was introduced whereby this competition was extended into the classroom, where an enormous wall-chart displayed the daily achievements of each team in such matters as attendance and punctuality, personal cleanliness and tidiness, politeness and helpfulness, as well as in games and academic subjects. On Friday afternoons all the points were added up, and the winning team of the week had an enormous coloured star marked in the appropriate position on the chart.

Chief rivals for the place of top team were the reds, of which I was a member, and the greens, captained by one Lloyd Williams, who was exceptionally good at games, and usually led his team to victory in all sporting events. However, we had the edge on them in the classroom, and a red star was often recorded. The blues did not fare quite so well, but occasionally made the grade through meticulous attention to detail and tidiness. The yellows, somehow, never managed to win at all. By virtue of some sort of staff bumbling when the teams were selected, no one in the yellows seemed to be any good at anything. If anyone was late, it would be a yellow. If anyone had dirty finger-nails, it would be a yellow. If anyone swore in class, it would be a yellow. Most of their English was atrocious and their arithmetic worse. They could not learn even the simplest poem by heart, or catch a ball, or touch their toes without bending their knees. A turn of phrase not then in common coinage would have designated them a dead loss. The powers-that-be conferred and decided that, for the purposes of morale, something must be done about the yellows. The result was a rehashing of the teams, and with tears pouring down my cheeks I informed my mother that I was to be Put-into-the-Yellows, who never, in any circumstances, won anything at all.

That the miracle worked was due not so much to me as to my mother, who diplomatically pointed out that if you cannot do arithmetic you can at least wash your hands and turn up on time, and her enthusiasm for the whole project began somehow to communicate itself to me and to my reluctant team members. They began to arrive at school early; they made Herculean efforts to keep themselves and their work clean and tidy. They even practised tunnel-ball in the playground and one day managed to win a game. I conducted much-loathed spelling bees in secret. I chivvied and coaxed and cajoled. It had never occurred to me before to assert myself quite so freely – in the reds there had been a number of strong personalities contending for leadership, and I was nowhere in the running. Now I was on the side of the underdog; missionary to the despised yellows. Consumed by a burning determination that we would win, I hurled myself into the battle. The pattern of my whole life was changing as I marched out of the shadow of my own shyness into the limelight of leadership.

Could I bring off a coup? Could the yellows be vindicated? In a final, rather desperate burst towards the end of term, the classroom swarmed with yellows, cleaning blackboards, emptying waste-paper baskets, dusting window-sills and arranging wild flowers in jam jars. Yellows, with shiny shoes and scrubbed faces, were first at their desks and last to leave them. Yellows, puffing with effort, were managing at last to make some sort of showing at games. It came, the last Friday of term, the hour of glory. A yellow star, brighter than any red, blue or green star had ever been, was ceremoniously affixed to the last space of the chart. Galloping home to share the glad news with my mother, I was aware only of my triumph and what I had gained. Maybe the slight wistfulness in her congratulatory smile concealed some sort of ache for the shy, dependent little creature who had been her child and who, it was obvious, would soon be gone for ever. For my part, I was conscious only that life was very exciting and very good. On the strength of my achievements I beat the local bully (a boy two years older than myself) in a fight the following week, and looked forward to the perpetual tribal warfare of the long summer holidays.

CHAPTER 4

War

THE word war does not convey a great deal of meaning to most five-year olds, and I was no exception. For some time I had been aware that all was not well in the adult world; that grown-ups talked increasingly of things I did not understand but which I sensed to be grave and terrible. The names of Hitler and Chamberlain became familiar and the Germans were frequently mentioned. I was unsure what the Germans were. When you live in a world inhabited by the pixies, the fairies, the gnomes and the goblins; when the borderline between reality and fantasy is still pleasingly blurred, and your extreme youth permits you to cross and re-cross that border without let or hindrance, then there is some difficulty in working out that while the gnomes or the goblins exist only in the fertility of your own imagination the French or the Germans are real. When the war first came, therefore, I was far more inclined to be afraid of the goblins than I was of the Germans, for I knew much more about the malpractices of the former.

My mother came into my bedroom that day, September 3rd, 1939, and informed me with what seemed to me rather an excessive solemnity, that we were at war. My lack of understanding must have reflected itself in my face, since she then proceeded to explain what war was. The explanation seemed satisfactory enough to me. Hitler and his minions were somewhere they had no right to be. Our soldiers were going to fight them and defeat them, and this appeared a perfectly reasonable proposition and a simple matter.

At first the pattern of life did not change very much. My evening prayers were extended to cover a petition for the safety of 'Uncle Harry and all the other soldiers, sailors and airmen'. Uncle Harry, my mother's brother and a great favourite of mine, was a regular in the Air Force and at the time the only member of the family considered at personal risk. I continued to make this petition throughout the six years of the war, despite a growing sense of the futility of its phrasing, though I tended to regard the survival of Uncle Harry as a strong mark of the power of prayer.

We were issued with gas masks, which I hated, mainly because the mica screen so quickly became steamy and prevented you from seeing out. Claustrophobia, a lifelong enemy, attacked every time I put the wretched thing on, and I felt as if not only my face, but my whole being were encased in that contraption of canvas and rubber. Regulations demanded that the gas mask must be taken everywhere, and although I often contrived to set off for school without mine, somewhere along the road one of my seniors always noticed its absence and despatched me post haste to fetch it, much to my chagrin. Worst of all, once or twice a week there came the detested gas mask drill, when suddenly, during a lesson, the teacher would shout "Gas" and the masks had to be put on and worn till further notice. I found that by appearing to support my head on my hands, with my elbows resting on the desk, during this period, I could insert my thumbs under the rim of the mask below my chin without being observed. This gave me a feeling of freedom since I could breathe more easily. What would have happened to me in the event of a real gas attack leaves little to the imagination, but survival of a gas-mask drill was of itself ordeal enough for me at that time.

My father joined the Local Defence Volunteers, which he always referred to as "Look, Duck and Vanish". At their first muster, they were supposed to take with them a weapon – any weapon upon which they could lay hands. My father at that time possessed a small shotgun, and took this for lack of anything better. He found himself among the better-equipped members. One local worthy had brought a hatchet – another the handle of his wife's broom. Fred Bartle, an elderly bachelor who lived a few doors away from us in The Gue, took a revolver, which he assured the company contained two shots. It had not, however, been fired for twenty years and my father gathered that the two shots had actually been in the gun during that entire period.

The LDV became the Home Guard, and my father, a First World War veteran, was put in charge of a platoon of young men. He took tremendous delight in training these boys, drilling them rigorously and marching them on Church Parades on Sundays. In between, he bemoaned the ineptitudes of his superior officers including the Vicar, Canon Gotto, and the local chemist, a man named Robins. They, in turn, endured the outspoken and insubordinate criticisms of my father, largely because he was the only senior man in the unit with any proper training in gunnery and without him they could not even assemble most of their equipment when it arrived. My father was in fact chosen by the War Office to blow up the Loe Bar Road in the event of invasion. This matter was so highly secret that he was not only forbidden to tell anyone where and how the explosion would be set off, but he was also debarred from admitting that it would be set off at all. Speculation was therefore rife in our immediate neighbourhood when one summer evening a rather imposing car drew up at the gate, and a high-ranking officer emerged. He proceeded to instruct my father in the matter of the explosives which had been laid and the position and timing of the fuses. Paying no particular attention to one small girl playing nearby, he let off a blank charge, which made an impressive bang, and my father then gave a repeat performance to show that he had understood the instructions. After some serious and intense conversation, the officer departed. Perhaps the best-kept secret of my whole childhood was that I, too, knew how to blow up the Loe Bar Road.

Watching the Home Guard drilling soon gave us a new game to play. A gun or a tin helmet was the top item on every boy's birthday or Christmas present list. An illicit trench, two feet deep, was dug in Paddy's Yard, and cursed by every adult who ever had cause to go there in the blackout. This trench, constructed with loving patriotism, became our home and headquarters. Everything took place in and around the trench. It was cookhouse, hospital and battleground all combined.

Real soldiers arrived in Paddy's Yard. I think they were from the East Yorks regiment but I cannot remember clearly. Certainly they were fêted as heroes, because they were the first troops we had ever encountered. Wide-eyed with adulation, we followed them wherever they went. They, in return, would sometimes give us a ride on a Bren gun carrier when there were no officers about, or at least permit us to climb aboard and peer out over the turret as though we were in battle. So, in the gathering clouds of the spring and early summer of 1940, we fought our own 'phoney war'.

Our first glimpse of the reality of the matter came on a Friday, one warm summer evening, when the first evacuees arrived. I remember the whole town seemed to have turned out to greet them, lining Fore Street as though visiting royalty were expected.

They came in a coach from Helston station, and disembarked at the end of Church Row, to be taken to meet the prospective 'aunties' in Church School. The sight of them is still a scar on my memory. Travel-stained and tear-stained, many of them had cried all the way from Paddington. Their eyes were red and swollen, and their cheeks, grimy with railway dirt, were streaked from crying. Many of them appeared to have no handkerchiefs, and sniffed, or wiped their running noses on the backs of their hands. All carried their gas-masks, grim reminders of the reason for their enforced visit. All had worn identity labels when they left home; some few had lost them and amongst these were a couple so frightened that they could not even remember their own names.

Holding tightly on to my mother's hand, I surveyed these children so recently separated from their own mothers. It was the first occasion in my life when I can remember experiencing the emotion I later learned to call pity.

Pity, however, soon gave way to a sense of shock, both for us children and for the grown-ups who had the harder task of fostering the evacuees. Here was an alien race come into our midst. To begin with, it was patently obvious that amongst the arrivals were a number from what the adults described as poor families. Their material poverty was evidenced by the inadequate way in which they were dressed and the pathetic little bundles of clothing they had brought with them. The day after their arrival was spent by a number of local women in shopping for new clothes or in finding decent quality cast-offs from local families, so that the waifs could be taken to Sunday school next day looking no less decent than the young strangers amongst whom they had come to live.

Getting used to living with the evacuees was one of the hardest adjustments we had ever had to make in Porthleven. Although few can have been aware of it at the time, it was a crucial turning-point in our world. To begin with, they were tough – tougher than any children I had previously met – tougher even than the boys from Gravesend Council houses, who had a reputation for

Little Nanspean. My first home

At three and a half months with Mother

1

Father haymaking

Mother

With Grandma

Grandma Giles feeding the chickens at Little Nanspean

2

With Teddykins at The Gue

Porthleven Beach in the 1930s
On the left: Auntie Maud Bowden and Rosa (back to camera)

St Peterstide, 1938 or 1939
Michael Rosewarne and I are in the foreground; behind us Symons' Ice
Cream van with Stanley 'Slabbie' Downing and his son Keith

With a friend

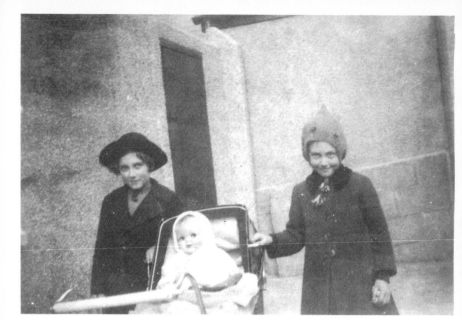

With Ann Gates and her dolls' pram. The pixie hood, hand knitted from odd scraps of wool, was fashionable winter headgear during the war. Ann is wearing her school uniform hat; she attended Miss Cox's private school in Helston.

The infants' class at Board School, 1938. Back row, standing: Robert Baxter, Barry Cowls, Rosemary Bawden, Margaret Williams, Joyce Russell, Muriel Pascoe, Willie Pascoe, Arthur Pascoe. Middle row, standing: Leslie Williams, Trevor Richards, Clive Williams, Russell Cowls, Jack Kitchen, Jennie Hosking, Elsie Giles, Dennis Oliver, Lloyd Williams, Keith Downing, John Vincent, Norman Pascoe. Seated: Marion Symons, Joyce Williams, Sylvia Orchard, Ross Bowden, Miss Mewton, Valerie Hosking, Loveday Hammill, Mabel Orchard, Dorothy Richards

The harbour from Peverell Terrace

Porthleven Harbour looking up to Breageside

Three of the Richards brothers aboard the Golden Rule

6

The ill-fated Energetic

*Charles Arthur taking a
lobster out of a net*

7

*The Friso coming through the gap. Notice the lack of space – great
precision was needed to bring the steamers through. On this occasion, the
ship was brought in by Charles Arthur, a local seaman, despite the captain
wanting to abandon her after an accident at sea during a blizzard.*

Charles Arthur, Ernest Toy, Willie Burgess, Edward Williams, Frankie
Rowe Bawden, Willie Waters

Porthleven fishermen
Left to right, standing: Arthur Orchard, Arthur Corner, Wallace Miners,
Tommy Matthews
Kneeling: Charles Arthur, Sammy Thomas, Isaac Brown

Michael Rosewarne in his smart new uniform for the Town Band, about 1948

9

Porthleven's first post-war football team, with committee and trophies.
Standing: Frank Strike, Tommy Strike, Reggie Pascoe, Stanley Oliver, Jack Thomas, Roy Richards, Jim Pawlyn, Joe Laity, Dick Goldsworthy, Leonard Reed, Harold Bray
Centre, seated: David Williams, Jim Ruberry, Jim Reed, Oliver Allen
Front, seated: Reggie Pawlyn, Eric Goldsworthy, 'Ollie' Miners, Teddy Johns, Willie Goldsworthy

St Peterstide around 1930.
The Peverell Road procession

Fore Street St Peterside procession. left to right: Harry Chesterfield,
Kenneth Bawden (with wreath) Alfred Pascoe, Lewis Mitchell, Joe Russell

The Peverell Road Banner setting out in the procession

11

Peverell Road procession. left to right: The Revd Christopher Jarvis, the Revd Gerald Williams, Mr Jim Miners, Mr Bill Reed, Mr Bobbie Jewell

Wartime fortifications on the cliffs near Loe Bar

Fishermen's memorial at Breageside

being the most unruly in the village. In the early days fights often broke out between the two camps, and whilst the Gravesend boys in general had the advantage of better nourishment and consequently better physique, plus the psychological superiority of being on home ground, the newcomers, inured to the continual struggle for survival in the East End of London – Bethnal Green to be precise – fought by their own rules, which approximated closely to those of the jungle. In addition they were touchy, being away from their natural territory, and thus easily goaded to anger. They were constantly under attack: the manner of their speech was held up to scorn and mockery; their tendency to be afraid of cows brought howls of derision, and the facts that numbers of them had head-lice or ringworm and that some of them, not unnaturally in the circumstances, persistently wetted their beds, were made occasions of public and humiliating insults. We were not kind to these strange children: we did not really know how to be kind to them, and even if we had, it is doubtful if they would have known how to respond to our kindness. They resented us – resented the fact that while they had been forced to leave their homes and be parted from their parents, we were still secure with ours – that the school to which they went was our school, not theirs; that we behaved with a maddening superiority and condescension, and talked in a strange tongue; most of all that we were utterly unimpressed with the fact that they came from London, which was the centre not only of their world, but of the whole civilised world, but did not appear to figure even remotely in ours. Thus the battle for playground supremacy continued over a period of months, and for the timid of both sides the beach became a place of terror throughout that summer, as bullies from each camp ranged about the tideline, ready to splash, duck and generally maltreat whatever victims they could find from the enemy camp.

My own first and only fight with an evacuee involved

57

a girl called Maureen Buckley, who was partially blind in one eye. Having waylaid me on a street corner, she belaboured me till I was forced into retaliation, and we fought like cats till we were both stiff with bruises, whereupon she burst into tears for the benefit of some adult passers-by, declaring that I had taken advantage of her defective sight in order to set about her and bully her. I retired mortified at my loss of honour, and formed a private opinion that whatever a German was like, he could surely not be much worse than an evacuee.

With the coming of autumn, however, the problems began to sort themselves out, and tempers cooled with the onset of winter. Classes were gradually integrated and we found ourselves sitting at the same desks as the young Londoners. Hesitatingly, the first overtures towards real friendship began to be made. We talked to one another, and laughed together when we could not understand each other's meanings. They told us about their parents, their older brothers and sisters or babies left at home: we gradually accepted them into our lives.

More evacuees had arrived during the summer, some in a private capacity and accompanied by relatives or parents: some from a Grammar School in West Ham, who shared Helston Grammar School for the duration. The number of pupils was too great for the accommodation, so a shift system was devised for lessons, and those who went to school in the afternoon and evening were often referred to as the night-shift – an idea which we all found immensely funny.

Among the private evacuees who came was a family named Gates. They were rather well-off and employed my parents to help them in the house and garden. They had a daughter, named Ann, who was only a little older than I was, and we struck up quite a friendship. I was able to introduce Ann to the life and customs of the village; she in turn shared her expensive toys with me and in general gave me a taste of a way of life I had hitherto not even dreamed about. Ann's bedroom was decorated entirely in pink – her own choice, and, from an adult point of view, probably quite repellent, but at the time I thought it marvellous. The furniture was pink; the walls were pink; even the sheets on the bed were pink. I had not known that such refinements as pink sheets existed. Ann also possessed a dolls' pram big enough to hold a real baby, and a Pekingese dog named George, who always came to stay with us when the Gates went away on holiday. Pekingese were never really my idea of a dog, but I adored George, and he thoroughly enjoyed his stays with us, partly because he loved running up and down stairs, and the Gates lived in a bungalow.

Mrs Gates was an invalid, and when she was particularly ill Ann herself would be sent down to stay with me for a few days. Not fully understanding the reason for these visits, we rejoiced in them, making them the occasion for tea-parties, picnics, and a succession of pillow-fights at bedtime, usually instigated by my father. We shared a tremendous enthusiasm for the countryside, and would walk miles together picking wild flowers and searching for birds' nests or toadstools, or whatever was in season.

We had just come in from such a walk one day, our cheeks glowing with the impact of the fresh air, clutching big bunches of rushes which we had gathered en route, when Ann's elder sister arrived to tell her that her mother had died. We sat, silently. I pretended to read a book, because I did not want to look at Ann's face. She did not cry at all, and I remember thinking how terribly brave she was. But there was no pillow-fight that night, and I felt upon me, for the first time in my life, that deep constraint which comes from needing to say something and finding no words available with which to say it.

Some of the evacuees were Jews. These seemed quite a distinct entity within the evacuee community, and for reasons which we did not then appreciate, evoked the special sympathy of the local grown-ups. They brought with them a religious instructor of their own, a Mr Goldbloom, who went around all the local schools teaching the Jews, and who came to us every Friday morning. His son, Jeremy, a solemn little boy with huge eyes, attended our infants' class and explained loftily that he did not come into morning prayers "because I am a Hebrew." There was a superb and indomitable dignity about the statement. Less dignified were the Hertzberg brothers, Gordon, Gerald and Bert, who possessed a quite fearful sense of humour and were always up to some awful practical joke. Gerald Hertzberg was on one occasion sitting behind Mabel in class, and cut her hair with his handicraft scissors. To make matters worse, he only cut one side of it, and she had to go home with a two-inch step in her hair. About this time, someone told me that Jesus had been a Jew. In my horrified imagination I wondered if He could ever have been anything like Gerald Hertzberg who was, in my rather priggish estimation, a wicked boy in spite of his grinning charm.

Gerald Hertzberg lived at a local farm, in the company of another evacuee, Harry Smith. Harry and his sister Edna had the most extreme of Cockney accents, and were even known by the local children as Harry and Edna Smiff. I became firm friends with the said Edna, and was with her on the famous occasion of the chapel Harvest Festival when she managed to drop her basket of fresh farm eggs onto the gravel in the yard, scandalising the adults on two scores: first, the disgusting mess of egg yolk in the sacred precincts, and secondly the shocking waste of good, scarce food.

Food rationing, source of so much worry and strain to our mothers, was no problem to us. After some slight initial surprise, we accepted the situation as natural; cheerfully ate margarine instead of butter; actually enjoyed dried egg and learned how to make our sweet coupons last the entire month by carefully apportioning them into weekly quotas. Choosing sweets became a simpler matter. Zoning had restricted the selection, and there was often only one kind you liked in the shop. Oranges and bananas disappeared almost entirely from the scene, except on very rare occasions when the arrival of a consignment would quickly create a queue reaching from Pascoe's fruit shop on the square to the junction of The Gue, one hundred yards further up the hill. Even then you had to produce either a baby's green ration book, or a schoolchild's blue one and have it stamped before your allocation of oranges was made. Some of the women in the queue would occasionally hand in a grey ration book. We discovered that anyone possessed of such a book was expecting a baby, and kept a hawk-like lookout for them in all the shops in order to be first with the news.

One of my mother's greatest food problems was the fact that my father persisted in filling the house with troops – some soldiers, but mainly airmen whom he met in the course of his war work at Predannack and St Eval airfields. Slightly too old to serve again in the Army, my father nevertheless became subject, as the war proceeded, to something known as an Essential Works Order, and travelled around the country driving vast pieces of machinery necessary for building and repairing runways. From time to time he was away from home for periods of up to two months. I loathed these occasions, and longed for his return home. As soon as he did, the flow of hungry airmen immediately resumed. My parents, like other local people, made a number of good friends in this manner, most of whom have turned up from time to time since, to renew acquaintance. Feeding them was a constant struggle for my mother, but she managed somehow, even going to the lengths of scalding the milk to obtain enough cream to spread on bread with home-made jam. I have no doubt that as the war drew to a close she mentally heaved a sigh of relief at the impending reduction in the size of her family. It was not to be, however, for as soon as hostilities had ceased, my father turned up to tea one day, beaming triumphantly as he ushered in a number of German prisoners of war, who sat around our tea-table like a gathering of Nordic gods, grinning benevolently and addressing me with incomprehensible questions, all of which seemed to end in "Ya". Some of them continued to visit us regularly until they were repatriated, and as their English improved and we grew to know each other better, I received my first lessons in international understanding.

The idea that one would soon entertain Germans in one's home was not, however, an acceptable one in the days of 1941 and 1942. These were the days of high patriotism; of Churchill's mighty speeches; of anguished wives and mothers with missing husbands and sons; of inveighing on street corners as to what should be done with Hitler and Lord Haw Haw when the war was won, and of songs, patriotic, or rude, or religious, sung defiantly in air raid shelters. Not that there was much need of air raid shelters in Porthleven: we had comparatively few alarms, which were mostly because of strays aimed at Falmouth Docks, fifteen miles away. Nevertheless, there were nights spent in cellars, with the throb of enemy aircraft overhead, and the persistent thudding of bombs dropping in the distance.

One local woman purchased an air raid shelter to fit under her kitchen-table. On one occasion when Falmouth was getting a rather bad raid, she was huddled in this claustrophobic contraption with her husband, her daughter, who was about my age, and several frightened neighbours. Space was at a premium. The sound of aeroplanes grew louder, and the thuds seemed near and frightening. The owner of the shelter began to pray aloud "Lord, come in here with us". The daughter, always of a practical turn of mind, retorted "Doan't ee go 'an invite no more in 'ere, Mother; we can't move nor turn now."

We had no proper shelters at school and in the event of a raid were expected to gather in the lobbies, which

62

were the part of the building most likely to be safe from blast. We were also walked in crocodile round the lanes and taught to throw ourselves into the hedges and on to the ground in the event of enemy aircraft opening fire. Occasionally, as a great treat, we were all rushed to the cellars of houses near the school, but this was not thought to be a very practical solution in the event of a genuine raid on the village. I hated the cellars anyway: they gave you an awful feeling of being entombed, and my constant fear was not that a bomb would fall upon us, but that I should be unable to escape from the cellars and reach my parents.

My anxiety to get home stemmed partly from the fact that I was never afraid when my father was present, possibly because the thing my father most detested was fear. He was the kind of man who would take you to the window during a severe thunderstorm to point out the beauty of the lightning, and scold you if you trembled. Likewise, during an air raid, he would peer excitedly at the sky to see if he could spot an enemy plane in the beam of the searchlight, and listen intently in order to be able to plot the exact position where the bombs might be falling. His lack of timidity came in very useful on Home Guard duty, when his patrol was required to stay overnight in a large, lonely house on the cliffs. This house, named Tye Rock after the part of the cliff upon which it was built, was reputed to be haunted by the ghost of Miss Woolfrey, the wealthy artist who had built it at the turn of the century. Most of the Home Guard boys were scared stiff of going into the place. Not so father, who remembered Miss Woolfrey from his childhood, and could not for the life of him see that the ghost of a lady who had often given him sixpence for opening her front gate when she wanted to ride through it on her horse would suddenly turn malevolently upon him when he was defending his country in time of war.

Before the Home Guard took Tye Rock over, it had

been leased by a gentleman who made a hasty and hushed departure after local fishermen had reported strange lights flashing seawards at night. The facts were never disclosed, but we were given to understand that he was a spy and were correspondingly thrilled at the knowledge. Tye Rock was left to the tender mercies of the Home Guard, and later of the Land Army, who were said to hold wild parties there, particularly at the time the war ended, but who did little to maintain the grounds, which went to wreck and ruin behind their clifftop fence of barbed wire. We were fortunate that, despite the defences on the cliff, we were still able to use our beach, apart from Loe Bar, which was heavily mined. A boy from Gunwalloe, out rabbiting with his dog, strayed into the minefield and was blown to bits, a tragedy which served to increase the respect the rest of us had for this dangerous area. During the invasion scare blockades were built across various roads in the village and remained there for the duration. Pill boxes appeared on the cliffs and some of them remained for many years to shelter ardent young couples from the worst of the weather.

Ardour, it seemed, was anything but daunted by the onset of hostilities. With the arrival of troops in the area, there followed the inevitable crop of engagements and weddings between them and local girls – another factor hugely instrumental in changing the face of the village, where before the war nearly everyone was in some way related to everyone else. Some of these marriages, resulting from rash behaviour in the blackout, were as doomed as local prognostication would have them to be; on the other hand a good many pillars of present Porthleven society are men who first came here as boys in war-time. Later, the Americans arrived, and carried away a few local girls as GI Brides. The Yanks were particularly popular with us children, for whom they gave comparatively lavish parties in the Public Hall, with presents and 'candy' all round. Best of all, we were each given a balloon to carry home – a luxury some of us had not seen since infancy. One of mine – an orange one – was so precious I refused to play with it lest it should be burst, and it dangled behind the bedroom door until in the fullness of time it perished and hung like a shrivelled mandarin on the end of its string. The Americans were also an unfailing source of chewing gum, and despite the threatenings of our parents we were never averse to waylaying them on street corners with cries of "Got any gum, chum?" to which piece of blatant begging there would be an unfailing response, usually of a most generous nature.

One day, towards the end of the war, Jimmy Squat had some chewing gum for sale in his shop, and we snapped this up very quickly. Our delight in our purchase made us reckless, and we surreptitiously continued to chew the stuff in class, much to the distaste of Griff, who was giving us a lesson on fossils that particular afternoon. The first offender was given a hundred lines to be written after school; the second two hundred and so on. I was amongst those caught late in the day, and given five hundred, rather to my consternation, since I was due to attend a friend's birthday party that afternoon. Griff was lenient, however, and I arrived at the party in time for tea, having got off with two hundred lines and a good scolding.

The strangest aspect of those six strange years was that they did not seem in the least strange to us. It was normal to carry a gas-mask; it was normal to go shopping with a ration book. It was even normal to have to turn out of bed occasionally and shelter till the all-clear sounded. Someone fell into the harbour in the blackout and was drowned. Someone's father was missing in the Far East. Someone was known to be getting meat on the Black Market. It was all quite normal. Someone's mother had come down from London on holiday, and to the disgust of the local mothers wore trousers and a great deal of make-up. But the local girls, too, were beginning to wear trousers and make-up. The unthinkable was becoming the accepted. We had salvage drives at school, with prizes for those who brought the most salvage. It was all collected in huge sacks and carried away to help win the war. Valerie Hosking got the first prize – a pink hair ribbon with blue spots, which I had coveted for myself. I resolved to collect even more salvage next time. Mars bars brought out a new advertising slogan: 'Cut it into slices and it goes further'. Some people even sandwiched it between bread, presumably to take the edge off the guilt they felt at eating such a luxury at all. We all joined the Junior Red Cross and learned to put arms into slings and hands and feet into bandages. You lost points for dropping your bandage and letting it roll across the floor.

Tommy Trinder came and made a film *The Foreman went to France*. We were offered the thrill of dressing up as refugees and going out in boat loads as extras. My mother unsportingly refused to let me go as it was a rough day and she feared I might be sick – which to do her justice I probably should have been. A Junkers crashed at the top of Chapel Downs and my father took me to see the wreckage. A bomb dropped in a field at Tregew Farm. Grand Concerts, Grand Socials and Grand Dances enlivened the evenings in the Public Hall, whither people crept through the dark winter evenings, their torches hooded in blue paper.

The sky over Falmouth became a gigantic aquarium, with barrage balloons moving restlessly like strange fish in its waters. Buses, with most of their seats removed, had the remaining seats turned sideways facing each other across an enlarged aisle where greater numbers of people could stand, "Move further up the bus, please," and you were frightfully sick on long journeys because of the diesel fumes. Men came and measured your height and the size of your feet at school to see if you ought to have extra clothing coupons because of your rapid growth rate. Essays were written on the backs of old

66

envelopes because the school had used up its term's small quota of proper writing paper. Strange men appeared in your friends' houses, and you were informed, with pride "This is Daddy." Some people's Daddies, you understood, wouldn't ever come back. In the evenings, you listened to Vera Lynn singing, or laughed at Tommy Handley's rude jokes, which you didn't quite understand, but everyone else seemed to find him funny so you did as well. Parcels arrived from relatives in America, containing new frocks, or a cake for Christmas. 'Dig for Victory' screamed the posters, and all the old men hurried to their allotments on Spring evenings. Uncles and cousins in uniform arrived to spend their leave, and you went to meet them at Helston station. Someone usually had to sleep on the sofa to make enough room in the house, and the grown-ups stayed up half the night swapping war stories. You would hear them as you lay in bed pretending to be asleep. At other times, you would hear the strange noise, half sawing, half singing, of father cleaning his rifle before going on Home Guard duty. The tones of Lord Haw Haw would decimate the silence of summer nights – "Germany calling, Germany calling," "OH SHUT HIM OFF, EDDY," and my father's laughter, confident, derisory. There was a war. One day it would be won. We would win it. Churchill said so. Daddy said so. What would it be like, not to have a war? What had it been like before the war came? How nice to have plenty of sweets. And oranges and bananas. I would eat oranges and bananas every day. And Mars bars, whole ones, not cut into slices. And walk about in the streets in the dark, looking at the lights in the windows. That would be nice. "Here is the news, read by Alvar Liddell . . . Enemy casualties were heavy when an offensive thrust was made . . ." – "Put that light out . . ." You were falling asleep in the blacked-out village, and it all seemed so perfectly normal. . . .

CHAPTER 5

Moppy and Methodism

VISITORS to Cornwall, while tending to admire the
magnificence of the coastal scenery, the splendour of the
moors and the quaintness of small villages, inevitably ask
the question "But what do you find to *do?*" as though
all community life and enterprise were doomed to perish
immediately upon crossing the Tamar. In fact, one of
the joys of life in a Cornish village is the absorbing and
sometimes demanding pattern of activity which dominates
one's leisure hours. The existence of such a pattern means
that there is always something to look forward to; always
the next thing waiting to be done; and boredom, for those
who will enter into the spirit of the thing, is an unknown
ailment. Even during the war years the old traditions were
kept alive somehow, and occasions like Helston Flora and
Porthleven St Peterstide were celebrated with as much zest
as ever, despite the fact that austerity might curtail the
style of a Flora-Day dress, or the number of currants in a
St Peterstide bun.

Summer began and ended in Helston. It began with
Flora Day; with children in white dresses and ladies in
long, flowered frocks, dancing behind the band through
the streets that were heady with the scent of the lily of
the valley. It ended with Harvest Fair, ripe with plums

and smelling of ponies and beer, when the gipsies came into town and got rolling drunk.

Between these two events came the high summer glory of St Peterstide, redolent of hot tea, saffron buns and squashy strawberries. The origins of this function go back beyond the recorded history of Porthleven into the dim days when blue-jerseyed fishermen were busy turning old net lofts into Methodist Meeting houses. Porthleven at that time had no parish church, and parishioners were expected to walk to Sithney or Breage for worship. It has been suggested that the original St Peterstide processions walked out to Sithney and back to celebrate the feast of St Peter, patron saint of fishermen. Cetainly the event has something in common with the *pardons* of Brittany. It also owes much, however, to the Whit walks in the North of England, and nowadays bears a singularly unflattering resemblance to a trade union demonstration. Influenced, no doubt, by all these factors, it nevertheless holds a special magic of its own, and Porthleveners living abroad always try to time their visits home to coincide with its celebration.

I have walked in every St Peterstide procession since I was three or four years old. Nowadays, there is one enormous parade of all the Christians in the town, accompanied by two or three bands and reaching at full stretch from the square almost to the town clock, a distance of around half a mile. In my childhood, however, St Peterstide was a wholly Methodist affair, and still retained a great deal of rivalry between the two large Methodist Societies, Fore Street, which I attended (commonly known as the Wesleyans) and Peverell Road, dubbed the Bryanites because of the influence of the evangelist O'Bryan in their history. Someone once told me that Bryanites always had hairs on their chests, and I used to view the lady members of their congregation with considerable suspicion on this score. In any event, it was not considered wise to mix the breeds, even at St Peterstide, and the marches took place on two consecutive days, June 29th and 30th in each year. June 29th was our day and we were very proud that it was the actual feast of St Peter in the church calendar, whereas Peverell Road had to content themselves with the 30th. They, on the other hand always contended that their day was a superior event, though in what respect I always failed to see, since the programmes for each were well-nigh identical.

In theory, we would assemble at the Sunday School at 2.30 on the day of the procession. In practice, it would often be about three o'clock before the majority of people arrived. In the commencement of public functions, Porthleven must be almost the tardiest place on earth. After further delay while we sang a hymn and someone prayed quite inaudibly against a babble of excited children's voices, we would march out round the town. An enormous Sunday School banner headed the procession, and it was and is considered a great honour amongst the young men to carry this object. In a high wind it can be exceedingly tricky to handle, demanding constant slackening and re-tightening of various ropes and tapes to keep it under control. Younger boys carried flags of various sizes and weights; Union Jacks; the flags of various foreign countries; or just flags, of no particular significance, but considerable gaiety and colour.

During the war, we often had to march without a band, and this gave rise to an extension of the custom of stopping to sing hymns at various junctures, a procedure we always found a little wearisome, as the old men would strike up the choruses over and over again. The march concluded in Kitto's field, an area normally used for the drying of nets, but which was specially cut and prepared for the occasion. Teas were served in an enormous marquee, and for those who preferred to bring a picnic, men went around the field with huge earthenware jugs of tea, which was bestowed, free, upon the picnickers. Brewed in ancient boilers over open bonfires, the tea was strong and smoky-tasting, and usually described as 'like bark', but nevertheless innumerable gallons of it were consumed, and this is a good indication of the quality of the brew. Children received an enormous saffron bun, the like of which it was supposed only a Cornish child could eat, but the evacuees soon developed an alarming capacity to enjoy saffron, and became as Cornish as the rest of us, at least for the day. Games and sports followed, the adults joining in, until dusk, when the bands would parade to the square and play more music.

Once or twice the circus came for the occasion, if circus is not too magnificent a word to describe two acrobats, a couple of clowns, a spangled equestrienne of uncertain age, an assortment of piebald ponies and a rather bored and elderly elephant. We paid a shilling each to watch the performance from hard wooden benches which were not even raised in tiers, so that those in the back rows had to be constantly moving their heads from side to side in order to see anything at all. On one occasion I was seated right at the back near one of the entrances, and during a trapeze act I heard a wheezing noise behind me and felt hot breath on the back of my neck. Turning round, I found that I was being subjected to the affectionate approaches of one of the piebalds, which placed me in the embarrassing position of not knowing whether to try to remove the animal, thus causing a tremendous disturbance, or to sit it out and hope that I would not be eaten alive. Fortune came to my aid in the shape of a circus hand who had noticed my plight and came round to remove the pony, but I was rather glad when the performance ended and I could escape to the comparative safety of the fairground.

The delights of the fair were always one of the high spots of St Peterstide. It was a small fair, held in a local field or sometimes on the harbour head. No one there was a stranger – we would greet the fairground children by their Christian names when they arrived each year –

they, in turn, knew us. Our parents would chat to their parents while we hurled coconut shys, swung in boats, or chased each other round in the dodgems. Dodgems are always so much more fun when you know everyone else on them. The whole thing used to become a kind of vast family party and the fun continued, fast and furious, till late into the night. You were not taken home early. It was St Peterstide; it was your day and you lived and enjoyed every last minute of it, even if you fell asleep over your mental arithmetic next morning.

It was only by accident that I was eligible for this Methodist fiesta, since it had been my parents' intention to bring me up an Anglican. Certainly the vicar regarded us as part of his flock, although his pastoral ministrations consisted chiefly of knocking at our back door and requesting the loan of the kitchen scissors, in order that he might cut the best of our arum lilies, which he regularly and shamelessly filched for the purposes of decorating the church altar on special occasions. My parents liked the vicar, but being low church, they were not at all happy with the Church of England in Porthleven, which was extremely high in its practice, and whilst they were dithering about the problem my mother was approached by a local Methodist lady with the suggestion that I might care to join the newly-established Primary Department of their Sunday School. Inspection proved this to be a well-run and pleasingly furnished unit and I was accordingly dispatched to it the following Sunday. From its sand tray (complete with camels to give a biblical effect) picture books and choruses, I graduated into the life of Methodism, which seen in retrospect was highly dissimilar from Methodism today.

I attended morning worship from the age of four, with Rosa, her father, (whom I always knew as Uncle Walter) and her younger sister, Shirley, who was really too young to be there at all, and made a great nuisance of herself during the sermon. The practice of taking young children out of church for that part of the service was unheard of at the time. We sat through five hymns, two lessons, two prayers, the notices, a children's address and a sermon. The hymns were often long and tedious; the prayers more so to a four-year-old, who had not the least idea of what being 'under the blood' or 'a sinner saved by grace' might mean. Fascination was lent to this aspect of worship, however, by the echoing Amens of the old men who sat around us at the rear of the chapel. Some of them, I noticed, would interject these at singularly inappropriate junctures, thus "Oh Lord Our God . . . Amen Amen . . . We thank Thee . . . Amen Amen . . . for all Thy mercies . . . Amen Amen," and so on. Occasionally, when much aroused, they would give vent to a hearty "Hallelujah," and strike up the verse of a hymn. I found this a confusing process, and never knew whether I must pick up my hymn-book and stand, or remain seated with my head bowed. I listened avidly, however, to the Bible stories, particularly those with which I was familiar from Sunday School, and for the most part enjoyed the children's address.

The sermon was an interval, usually rather too long, when Uncle Walter would produce hot peppermints from his jacket pocket, and when, provided you kept quiet, you could think your own thoughts and let your mind wander where it would. One of my favourite occupations at this time was 'opening the doors'. The rostrum at the front of the chapel bore a carved design upon it, which resembled a row of ornate, panelled doors, all firmly closed. I found that by intense concentration one could wander into the hall where they stood, and open them, one by one. Behind them were rooms elaborately furnished in red velvet or pink satin or, if the preacher had been reading from the Book of Revelation, paved with gold and studded with pearls. Sometimes there would be a golden throne, too, though I refused to contemplate the image of a Lamb upon it. Lambs belonged gambolling in fields or, as fat cardboard cut-outs, in the window of Mr Wimbleton's butcher's shop. Thrones were occupied by kings – by God perhaps, but never by lambs.

On rare occasions we sat upstairs in the gallery, and this gave imagination a new outlet during the sermon, when if you stared hard enough the well of the chapel would fill with water and become a vast pool, into which you could dive and swim. Or a tight rope might be fastened across the gallery from one side to another, and heroically you could run across it, dressed like the fairy lady you had seen at the circus. The munchings and wrigglings of Shirley quickly brought you back to earth, however. If the sermon were particularly long and dry, Uncle Walter would surreptitiously make a cracker or a mouse from his handkerchief, and we learned to perform this feat for ourselves, rushing the mice up and down the hymn-book stand, the seat, and each other's laps.

There was no knowing when the service would end: sometimes it seemed interminable, and again I would be seized with the panicky feeling that I might never be returned to my parents. This fear was intensified when at the close of the final hymn the preacher might say "Will some brother lead us in prayer?" This would be a signal for at least three old men to stand up in sequence and pray passionately for about five minutes each. I hated these prayers. They frightened me. I wanted them to end: I wanted to go home.

Nevertheless, I spent many of my happiest hours on Methodist premises, where there always seemed to be something of interest going on. High in the ranks of these events stood the Faith Tea, a remarkable institution, the chief feature of which was that you brought food with you and then paid to eat it. Not surprisingly, these teas made quite a bit of money for church funds: perhaps more surprisingly, particularly in view of rationing, people supported them with enthusiasm and vied with one another in the generosity of their contributions. Sponges made with real eggs would appear on the tables, alongside home-made saffron and yeast buns, to say nothing of fruit cake and the inevitable splits with jam and cream. These goodies would vanish like snow before the sun, as aproned, bosomy ladies with enormous teapots dispensed cup after cup of tea at the ends of the long tables. Faith teas, besides being held in their own right, formed an ancillary part of various other functions. Thus at the spring festival there would be Faith tea and daffodils, the drabness of the schoolroom transformed by the massed yellows of spring flowers. Or for the autumn effort: Faith tea and home-made stuffed toys, knitted golliwogs, kettle-holders (suitable for Christmas presents) made from odd scraps of material, and weird blocks of soap which were made, apparently, by compressing odd ends together in jars.

Then there were the concerts, almost too numerous to mention, always 'Grand' on the posters and sometimes rather chaotic in performance. Concerts by male-voice choirs; concerts by concert parties from other chapels in the district; concerts by the guild; concerts by the Sunday school children, rehearsed by harassed teachers who were never sure if anyone would know their lines in time. All played to packed audiences, whose enthusiasm alone was enough to raise the spirits and the standard of performance of the veriest amateur. The ladies of the church presented a play 'The Gift of the River God' – about the infant Moses – and decorated the stage charmingly with pampas grass filched from the local recreation ground. The men, not to be outdone, performed 'Joseph and his Brethren' in woollen dressing gowns and striped towels fastened round their heads with old neckties. The stage curtains were rose-pink and were not quite wide enough to meet in the middle. If you placed yourself in the right position in the audience, you could see through the crack before each scene started and inform your neighbour that there was "Uncle Walter dressed up" on the stage. The really venturesome could sit themselves in that part of the gallery which overlooked the stage behind the curtains, and thus obtain a complete preview of all proceedings, but this was greatly frowned upon and considered unsporting.

The youth club, formed during the war, broke fresh dramatic ground one winter with a presentation of a full-length dramatised version of *Scrooge*. They procured, for this major production, proper stage lighting and the services of a make-up artist. Scrooge, on viewing himself in a mirror for the first time, was promptly sick, and it is hard to say whether this was a compliment to the skill of the make-up man or not.

About the same time the youth club obtained a sound film projector, and amid great controversy started to show 'good quality' films in the Sunday school. It was deemed necessary by the trustees that these films should be religious or at least improving in content; one of the most popular was *The Great Mr Handel*, with whose moments of musical revelation we all became rather boringly familiar. At Christmas time there were the socials, when the forms were cleared from the schoolroom floor, and everyone assembled to play traditional games, including 'Oyster Sir' and 'A hunting we will go'. These games, most of which involved kissing one's partner to an accompaniment of ribald applause, tended to find great favour with the teenagers of the day, and were a useful substitute for dancing, which at that time was not permitted on the premises. One year the minister's son introduced a new game which was played with great gusto, it seems, by all and sundry. Its name was the Hokey kokey. Unfortunately, the next morning some of the trustees discovered that the Hokey kokey was in fact not a game at all, but a dance, and a major scandal arose.

I was not really old enough at this time to appreciate the niceties and nuances of kissing games. Tender relationships with the opposite sex did not greatly enter one's thinking. True, a boy might suddenly kiss you if you were hiding together in a dark place in the course of a game, and you would both giggle and blush terribly and say no more about it. One or two of the more squalid types at school might occasionally make a grab at the hem of your skirt, hoping to ascertain the colour of your knickers, but such behaviour was invariably greeted with such howls of protest and concerted scratching, hair-pulling reprisals by all the girls in the vicinity that the offender usually beat a hasty retreat. Even our games of fathers and mothers were totally sexless. Fathers went out to work or to war and remained there for the duration of the game, while the mothers bathed and dressed their dolls and prepared invisible meals for their non-existent spouses.

On the whole we were not very interested in the Fathers and Mothers type of game, preferring something more active and violent. One of the great favourites was Moppy or Mobby. There are numerous versions of this game: the one we usually played involved gathering round a convenient telegraph-pole or gatepost, which was known as the moppy post. A ball was then thrown into the air, and someone's name would be called. While this player was catching the ball, the rest would run away as fast as they could to strategic points of cover, stopping immediately the ball had been caught. The object of the game was then to creep back home to the moppy post without being hit by the ball, which could be thrown at any selected victim. To enjoy the real flavour of this game it should be played at dusk, when it is hard to see the ball, and hard to see the creeping shadowy figures sliding along walls and gutters towards the moppy post. Moppy, late on a smoky October afternoon, followed by kippers for tea, eaten by the first fire of the season, might have been the best description I could have given of heaven when I was eight years old.

Sometimes at weekends and during the holidays my father would take me to Penrose, and I regarded these outings as a tremendous treat. While it could by no means qualify as a stately home – indeed the mansion house itself is a rather squat, uninteresting piece of architecture, at any rate from the exterior – Penrose was large and imposing enough to make itself the setting of many a childish dream of grandeur in the village, while the acres of woodland in which it was set, sloping down to the banks of Loe Pool, Cornwall's only real lake, became to me a kind of paradise, entry to which could never fail to thrill. In spring there would be primroses, followed later by a carpet of bluebells, so thick you could not walk between them without crushing them. That you were not permitted to pick these flowers mattered not a whit – there were, after all, plenty of hedgerows where you could pick flowers – but it was only in Penrose that you could feast your eyes on such an abundance of them. In summer everything grew lush, and if you walked in the woods after a windy night you would be almost overpowered by the bruised, green smell. In summer, too, the yellow flags came into bloom around the marshy edges of the Loe, and the pink and white water-lilies coloured the surface of the pool. This was the best time of year to visit the gardens, and I was fortunate in that, during the war years, those gardens were placed in the charge of my uncle Jim.

Uncle Jim was my father's brother, but he was twenty years older than my father, and therefore seemed to me more like a grandfather, with his bristling grey moustache and his quaint, old-fashioned manner of dress and speech. For work he always wore breeches and leggings, disdaining denim overalls and such-like modern frivolities. His shirts were usually of cream flannel or twill, with a fine stripe in them, and collarless. On high days and holidays he would wear a detachable collar, but he dispensed with such unnecessary restrictions during working hours. His only method of transport was an elderly, but well-maintained bicycle and he went everywhere on this machine, cutting rather an odd figure at times when he was dressed in his best black jacket and bowler hat, complete with a rose in his buttonhole. He always made a tremendous fuss of me when I went to see him at Penrose and would allow me to sample every edible thing that was in season, including peaches, nectarines and grapes from the hot-houses, tomatoes, pears, green peas and of course, all the varieties of eating apple. I particularly loved the russets, with their golden-brown skin and rather nutty flavour. On one occasion Uncle Jim gave me a fig, which had ripened reasonably well on the tree in the corner, but I did not really care for it and was glad to be offered a pear instead.

The gardens at Penrose had a smell that was entirely their own – a smell composed partly of the earthy scent of good, warm, crumbly soil; partly of the blackberry-jam sort of smell of the sun on pine trees, and partly of the blue, acrid aroma of Uncle Jim's pipe.

Perhaps the best time of all to visit Penrose was on a cold, dry afternoon, in autumn, when the low sun would slant through the trees on the carpet of fallen leaves, and you could shuffle your feet through them and they would crackle joyfully beneath your tread. On those days you would see the red squirrels which, like you, were after the chestnuts. My father had spent much of his boyhood on the estate, and had worked there as assistant woodman before the First World War; consequently he knew where all the best chestnut trees were to be found, and we would creep, a pair of delighted conspirators, away from the main paths where the public were permitted to walk, through forbidden territories, along badger runs and into secret places in the woods, probably only known to about a dozen people, for me to fill my basket with nuts. My fingers usually got stiff with the cold, and I would prick them on the sharp cases, but the prize was worth the effort; sitting round the fire that evening, we would roast chestnuts on the bars till they sizzled and spat out, and I would let the uncooked ones run through my fingers, marvelling at the texture and colour of their skins, which for me are the epitome of autumn.

Once or twice during the year we would visit my Uncle Henry at Devoran. Uncle Henry, like his brother Jim, worked as a gardener on a large country estate: unlike Uncle Jim he actually lived on the premises, in an enchanting picture-book cottage with the sort of front garden you normally only see on calendars. This garden was in fact kept by his wife, Aunt Minnie, who worked on the basic principle that if you cram into the available space as many varieties of plant as you possibly can, then there will be no room left for weeds. So throughout the spring and summer forget-me-nots, wallflowers, tulips, stock, antirrhinum and asters jostled for position with masses of aubretia and snow-on-the mountain and pansies, the whole backed by enormous hollyhocks growing up the walls and even more enormous lilac bushes across the stable yard. The stable gave me great delight, even though during the war it contained no horses, but I would spend hours there examining the harness, the brasses, the rosettes and prize-tickets of bygone champions.

Uncle Henry was rather a round man, very like my grandmother in appearance. He was distinguished by having only one ear, the other one having been bitten off by a playful puppy when he was a small baby. He told us that before that incident he had been sickly, though after it he thrived, so perhaps he owed the dog something in spite of his injury.

Devoran was a very difficult place to reach by bus, and for this reason we could not visit Uncle Henry as often as I, for one, would have liked, for I loved both the man and the place.

School holidays in those times of restricted travel tended for all of us to be unbroken by many outings or excursions, and thus they became breeding grounds for mischief. There was, for instance, the day of Miss Bartle's fence. Miss Bartle, sister and housekeeper to her elder brother,

Fred (the same Fred Bartle who had taken his revolver to the first muster of the Home Guard) and to her younger brother, Percy (who wore plus-fours and carried a walking-stick with a silver knob) spent most of her spare time working in a very neat garden in front of her house just down the road from ours. It was indeed a most interesting garden, containing a conservatory with various exotic plants, including a magnificent oleander. It was also distinguished as the habitat of the only tree in The Gue, an ash, the annual life-cycle of which I watched with loving concern for many years. Around the garden was a wooden fence, mounted on a low wall, and having vertical bars about one inch thick and three inches apart.

August was very sultry that year. It was not conducive to flying up Peverell Terrace in a Spitfire shouting "Eeeow" and other appropriate noises. It was unsuitable for beaching since rain threatened continually. It was an August for chalking messages on walls, or bouncing a ball lethargically, or sprawling on the pavement trying to think of something cool to do. On such an occasion Pauline Chegwidden, Michael Rosewarne and I found ourselves seated staring across the road at Miss Bartle's fence. Miss Bartle was not about. Michael wandered idly across and ran his hand along the fence. The bars rattled like loose teeth. You could easily knock them out with a pot-shot. It would be quite fun.

One by one we took aim. You had to be careful. The ball might go through the bars into the garden and you might be caught fetching it, in which case the ball was certain to be confiscated and you would be reported to your parents. Miss Bartle was a stickler for discipline and not over fond of children. But Miss Bartle remained conveniently out of the way. One by one, the loose teeth were knocked away, leaving the parallel horizontal bars of the fence like a gummy grin. Panic seized us. Supposing we were found out and sent to prison? In an agony of terror we rushed into the garden, gathering up the fallen bars. Feverishly we replaced them in the rotten sockets. Some of them refused to go in properly. We did the best we could, propping them up against one another. The road remained quiet. No one emerged to confront us. We crept away to Paddy's Yard, smothering our guilt complexes with giggles. A short time afterwards, the fence was replaced by a double row of concrete blocks. Temptation was removed, and with it the view into quite the prettiest garden in the road.

'Getting up to roguery' was an aspect of childish behaviour largely accepted and winked at by adults in Porthleven, many of whom delighted in regaling us, from time to time, with stories of outrages perpetrated in their own faraway youth. Spurred on by these tales, we strove to emulate them. We locked the Youth Club in the Sunday school one night, causing considerable consternation. We deposited 'parcels from America' containing stones and rubble from Ching's granite works, in the porches of various recipients. Our forged postmarks and stamps, carefully steamed off letters from relatives in America, must have been skilful enough to deceive at least a proportion of our victims, for we heard shrieks of rage from their houses as they discovered the contents of the packages. We knocked at doors and gave false messages: "Mrs So and So wants to see you at *once*," in breathless voices, amd concealed ourselves, giggling, to hear the results. We found that we could ease the lock of one of the garages in Paddy's Yard, and having gained access, could crawl through holes in the partitions to every other garage in the row. In one of them we discovered an unlocked trunk containing a number of evening dresses and some curtains, enabling us to give an impromptu costume play, which, however, had to be interrupted by intervals of absolute silence whenever anyone came into any of the other garages. The incident which most nearly landed us in serious trouble, however, was one which was conceived with no malice aforethought.

It was, we thought, a brilliant idea that we should set up our own fairground in The Gue, to operate throughout the holidays. It would give the rest of the village children something to do, and keep them out of mischief. All that morning we scavenged for suitable small objects to give away as prizes, and racked our brains contriving stalls and sideshows. The final result had a creditable appearance. A dartboard (three throws for a halfpenny) was a centre of attraction. This was flanked by hoop-la on one side and skittles on the other. Small children could have rides in the rocking-boat, the mudguard of an old lorry abandoned in Paddy's Yard. Word spread round the village that we were opening after lunch, and a positive swarm of customers quickly arrived in response to our choruses of "Roll up, roll up." Halfpennies flowed like water. Soon all the prizes we had provided had been won, and we dispatched a couple of helpers to a local shop to purchase more with the takings. They returned with small toys, pencils, crayons and also cigarettes, which they had illicitly bought for themselves, much to our fury. Business continued brisk, however, and we were on the point of replenishing the prizes yet again when one or two suspicious parents began arriving on the scene. Uproar ensued. Our hard-earned store of halfpennies was, it seemed, ill-gotten gain and must immediately be redistributed to all those who had paid. But there arose the question of the prizes. We could not return them to the shop. Many of those who had won them had gone home to other streets anyway, and we could not remember who had spent how much. The venture ended ignominiously with all remaining prizes and all our takings being divided between those customers who remained to stake their claims. It was our first introduction to the irksome restrictions surrounding big business.

Baulked of our fairground, we were at least successful in our carnival. We elected a carnival queen, dressed her in a white silk dress borrowed from somewhere or other, and crowned her with marigolds. Her float, decorated with the hydrangeas which grew like weeds in the corner of every backyard, was a soapbox on wheels known as a butt. Every boy in Porthleven tried to own a butt, and boys in The Gue, in particular, risked life and limb to race these precarious vehicles down the steep, one-in-four slope from Peverell Road. If they felt generous they would give you a ride on these occasions, which was a big thrill, though you might well fall out and skin your knees. On the day of the carnival, however, they did not race, but proceeded sedately as befitted the occasion. We all dressed up; one or two boys blew toy trumpets and banged drums, and most of the adults were gracious enough to turn out to cheer the procession as it wended its ceremonial way from 'Up Under' to Paddy's Yard, where prizes of sweets were presented.

During the same summer of the fair and the carnival, we held the dog shows. It is hard to remember what caused the sudden popularity of this form of entertainment, but it suddenly became imperative to have a dog – if you did not own a dog, then to borrow a dog, in order to take it to the dog shows. We held these, by common consent, in the field behind the Vicarage. A ring was staked out, and small jumps erected, with other obstacles which the dogs had to negotiate as part of their tests. Most of the contestants were spaniels; my own candidate was a plump bitch named Sally, who really belonged to Michael Rosewarne, but he in turn always borrowed his uncle's trained gun dog, Bruce, who was much better behaved than Sally and usually won first prize. Mabel had the misfortune to adopt another spaniel, Peter, whose owner, a Mrs Williams, was universally known as Emma Cook.

Emma Cook loved Peter dearly, but could not control him very well, and Mabel found that he was not particularly responsive to her, either. Bruce would leap gracefully over the obstacles; Sally would go under or around them; Peter would knock them over. Bruce would run smoothly at the end of his lead; Sally would puff heavily behind: Peter with a glint in his eye, would slip his lead if at all possible and dash off in the wrong direction. When his outrageous behaviour was reported to her, Emma Cook would scold him beneficently, addressing him as "Old Ragged Ass" and feeding him titbits the while. She was a lonely woman, and he was literally her best friend. He died an untimely death, and was mourned by us all. There were no more dog shows after that, and when the war ended they built bungalows in the field behind the Vicarage, so that now you cannot even point to the spot where we used to hold them.

I loved animals, though having been removed in infancy from the farm atmosphere, I had grown timid of the larger ones and always treated cows and horses with respect. Nothing pleased me more, however, than to spend a day at a farm. There were two which we usually visited each school holidays: Tangies and Medlyn Moor. The latter, farmed by my father's brother Norman, was situated in the middle of wild moorlands off the Falmouth road, and could only be reached by traversing a long, muddy lane which runs across country between Halwin and Polgrane. It was impossible, except in the hottest and driest spells of summer, to negotiate this lane at all without wearing wellington boots, and in the winter it was quite likely that even these would become bogged down in the mud and only be extracted with extreme difficulty.

A visit to Medlyn Moor, therefore, would take on something of the aura of a military operation. Wellingtons and old mackintoshes must be taken, but it was not done to appear in these on the bus, so they had to be packed in a large bag for use on arrival. Another bag would contain slippers and dry socks. A third would be stocked with food; either a home-made cake or some corned beef, with perhaps some fruit and tomatoes. It was considered discourteous, in wartime, to go visiting for a whole day without taking with you at least a small contribution to the meal, even though your hostess usually spent the first half-hour after your arrival in scolding you for bringing it. This, however, was a matter of form; when she arrived to visit you she would be similarly laden with edible gifts, and it was your turn to scold her.

In order to reach the farm by a reasonable mid-morning hour, you had to leave home by about nine o'clock, and queue for a bus which departed from the square at ten. The hour spent in the queue was a very boring one, but if you came later it was by no means certain that you would get on the bus at all.

The journey, twisting about the lanes between Trenear and Porkellis, was tedious and by the time we disembarked at Halwin I often felt extremely sick because of the diesel fumes which permeated the atmosphere. Half an hour's safari across the moors was usually sufficient to revive me, however, particularly when Uncle Norman turned up at the end of the lane with the horse and cart, proffering rides. The grown-ups usually declined this honour; the cart was a crude thing with nowhere to sit down except on the floor between the empty milk churns, but I regarded it as a bold and adventurous undertaking, especially when on arrival at the cart-house the horse was taken from the shafts and the cart would bump forwards with alarming ferocity, so that you had to grab wildly at the sides to prevent yourself from being tipped out.

My uncle Norman vastly enjoyed teasing us in this way. He had a great sense of humour and loved children: I thought he was marvellous. He intrigued me by always wearing his cloth cap back to front, and he assured me solemnly that he did this to stop the flies from biting the back of his neck. He had one of the most interesting speaking voices I have ever heard, deep and husky, yet smooth and satisfying, rather like the purring of a contented tiger. Indeed, I believe he was quite a contented man, though sometimes the tiger beneath the surface would show, particularly when he and my father began to argue about politics. He was a staunch Conservative; my father a passionate Socialist. They would shout and storm at one another for what seemed like hours until, when you despaired of their ever calming down again, one of them would make the other laugh, and to everyone's surprise they always parted the best of friends, each vowing to make the other see sense at their next meeting.

I had two cousins at the farm, Lily and Christine. Lily was twelve years older than me, and seventeen years older than her sister. I always regarded her as grown up and looked up to her accordingly, tending to follow her about when she was there, which was seldom enough, since she was usually out at work most of the day, so I saw little of her. It was left to Christine to entertain me, and this she did in a fashion entirely her own. She was one of those children who by virtue of having been brought up with animals are totally fearless of them, and we therefore spent our time wandering about cowsheds, piggeries and the back legs of the horse, she entirely confident and myself trembling within but determined not to show fear in the presence of one so much younger than I. We were usually accompanied on these expeditions by a collie dog named Keeper, distinguished by having one brown eye and one china-blue one, which gave him a rather strange look, and I stood in considerable awe of him, though he was a gentle enough beast when you got to know him.

Christine also owned a cat, which rejoiced in the name of Kidney. This remarkable animal was in the habit of permitting itself to be dressed in dolls' clothes and wheeled about in a pram. One day Christine decided to demonstrate this achievement to me, and we set out down the lane from the farm, the pram bumping wildly over the potholes and the cat, complete with dress, bonnet and shawl, peering out from under the hood. Whether it was uneasiness at my presence, or Christine's unduly rough handling of the pram that morning which disturbed her, we never knew, but Kidney decided that she had had enough. Leaping from the pram, she jumped across the stream into a field, and we stood and watched her streaking away into the distance, dress and shawl flying out behind her, for all the world like a character from a Beatrix Potter book come to life. She returned several hours later with her clothes in a somewhat tattered condition!

Our own condition after a morning roaming the farmyard and wading through the muddy stream at the bottom of the lane usually left much to be desired, and considerable cleaning operations were required before we were fit to sit down to lunch. There was no such thing as a piped water supply to Medlyn Moor. Water came from a well at the side of the house, an immensely deep, dark shaft in the ground, with hart's tongue ferns growing out of the stones around its sides. It was worked by a windlass, and I liked to turn the handle of this, even though I had a secret fear of falling into the well, and indeed had a recurring nightmare throughout my childhood in which this actually happened. But the water was cold and clear like the moors on a frosty morning and it was marvellous to watch the sunlight sparkle and dance on it as the bucket finally swung its way to the surface. It was also, I remember, bitterly cold water in which to wash, but wash in it we did, in an enormous earthenware bowl which stood on an old backless chair just inside the kitchen door. There was always an enormous cake of Lifebuoy toilet soap, and the strong, hygienic smell of this would mingle strangely with the aroma of cooking as we dried our hands on the striped towel which hung on a vast wooden roller behind the door.

There was usually a roast chicken for lunch. A succulent, brown chicken, which had lived its life in the open air and been plucked and dressed by Aunt Dora's own hands. A flavourful, melt-in-the-mouth chicken, roasted slowly and to perfection in the oven of the slab; a chicken fit for royalty, the like of which I suppose even royalty rarely taste nowadays. This would in all probability be followed by an apple or blackberry pie, with clotted cream made in the kitchen that very morning. You tended, on these occasions, to forget that such a thing as rationing existed, and to stuff yourself until you could hardly move.

But there were so many things to do. Usually, we fed the hens, and once, at Easter, I was allowed to hold an egg in my hand while the chick hatched from it. It was a poor, wet, bedraggled thing, but beautiful in my eyes, and I was reluctant to let it go to be warmed by the kitchen stove. Sometimes there would be kittens in one of the barns, and we would make frequent trips to see how they were getting on. In the summer, when the harvesting was being done in the fields, we would carry out a big jug of tea and some cake to the men. For our reward we might have a ride back on the wagon, if we were lucky. In winter, when it was often too wet and muddy to go out, we would pass away the afternoon playing records on an ancient gramophone in the sitting-room. Part of the charm of this thing was that you had to keep winding it up or the record would slur into a ghastly travesty of the tune it was supposed to be playing, and we vied with one another to grab the handle in time to prevent the entertainment from flagging. By tea-time, on those winter days, the oil lamp would be lit; this was a treat in itself. Sitting there in the soft lamplight, listening to the wind sighing continually outside the house, I no longer wanted to play, or even to talk. From the settle in the corner of the kitchen I would watch the light playing on the brass knobs of the oven door, and the shadows flickering spookily in the far corners of the room. Uncle Norman could make animal shadows with his fingers, and sometimes he would do this to amuse us after tea. We awaited these shows with all the eagerness displayed by a modern child for its favourite television programme.

Walking back up the lane in the dark was another adventure. Uncle Norman would come with us, carrying a hurricane lantern in defiance of the blackout, though the light it threw was infinitesimal. However, it was certainly better than the feeble glimmers from our covered torches, and we would contrive to reach the main road without falling into too many puddles. Occasionally, as a great treat, Uncle Dick's taxi would be waiting at the top of the lane to take us home. Uncle Dick was another of my father's innumerable brothers, and his taxi was in great demand at that time. It was an Alvis, a huge, old-fashioned, cavernous affair, with an enormous angular bonnet and an uncompromising square end. My great delight was to ride on the little folding seats which it contained for the accommodation of extra passengers in an emergency. One dark night, however, I became over-exuberant at the thought of riding on the said seats, and fell out through the back door, which had not been properly shut. Luckily the car was not moving; indeed Uncle Dick was still walking about outside: I fell at his feet, grazing both hands and knees in the process, and he, surprised in this fashion in the pitch darkness, stepped on me for good measure, ensuring bruises which were the envy of all my friends for days afterwards.

I was never really able to love Medlyn Moor, even though I spent so many happy hours there. It was a dank, depressing sort of place. Pennyworts and innumerable mosses and ferns grew from outhouse walls, lending an air of decaying age. Sluggish streams ran in from the moorlands, oozing their tired way through earth that was black and sodden for most of the year. The farmhouses in the area had a weary, exhausted look: exposed as they were to every wind that blows across that bleak tract of moor, their windows were as few and as small as possible. This made them dark and claustrophobic within. Their gardens were practically non-existent, although in places hedges of escallonia or myrtle would shelter small beds containing a few wallflowers, pinks, nasturtiums and the odd hardy chrysanthemum or two. But it was a cold place, often shrouded in white mist, the accusing fingers of the disused engine houses pointing from the skyline into the clouds.

Tangies, the other farm we used to visit, was a very different proposition. Tucked into the side of the valley running between Carminowe and Loe Pool, it was gentle and sunlit and warm. Tangies was the sort of farm you see in a child's picture book. The cream-washed farmhouse had even creamier roses growing in a thick arch over the front door. These roses always seemed to be in flower, even late into the winter. Cats, sunning themselves on the doorstep, would purr and rub against your legs as you went in. The kitchen was a warm and well-polished version of all farm kitchens: a slab, with a high mantelpiece over, housing a pair of china dogs; a glass-fronted cupboard with the best cups and a few precious ornaments and favours from people's wedding cakes: an elderly wall-clock with a loud, slow tick: a settle, with its back to the entrance, from which you could see out into the farmyard and the fields beyond; a door, leading to the slate-floored dairy at the back, and another door, looking for all the world as though it were a cupboard, concealing the staircase. The accessories to this sort of room invariably included a calendar from a firm of agricultural merchants in Helston, and several sticky fly-papers, upon which you could watch with horrid fascination the death-struggles of house-flies, bluebottles and wasps.

They kept two horses at Tangies; Blossom and Madam. Blossom was a lumbering old mare whom I loved to ride. You had no need of a saddle or reins when riding Blossom. Sitting on her vast, broad back – so broad that your legs stuck out almost at right-angles to your body – and holding on to her mane, it was an easy matter to communicate to her where you wanted to go, and she would go there in the most docile and obedient fashion. Madam, her daughter, was aptly named, and no amount of persuasion could induce me to mount her. She was a stamping, head-tossing, capricious beast, and even to catch her and put a halter on her necessitated rushing around like a sheepdog in diminishing circles, hoping that she would tire before you did, which unfortunately was not always the case.

Occasionally there was a donkey to ride at Tangies, and I loved this best of all. The donkey was owned by a certain Walter Hosking, who lived at Porthleven and was a thatcher, the last man in the village to follow that trade. He came regularly to Tangies to cut withies, and was consequently often there when we visited; on one occasion we rode back into Helston with him in the donkey-cart, and I could not have felt more honoured if the king had offered me a lift in one of the state coaches. I begged my parents to buy me a donkey of my own, but the lack of grazing facilities and stables was gently pointed out to me and I was dissuaded. My enthusiasm for animals was a continual problem to my parents, since we had no real room to keep pets in our small house; eventually they compromised by buying me a canary for my eighth birthday.

I named him Peter, and he lived till I was eighteen, singing lustily morning, noon and night throughout his ten years of life.

The great activity in Tangies during the summer holidays was blackberry picking, for the fields that lie around the shores of the Loe Pool are rich in this delectable fruit. We always dressed in wellingtons for these expeditions, even when the weather was hot and dry, to protect our bare legs from scratches. We never wore trousers; it was unheard-of for little girls to wear trousers, though I was permitted to have a pair of shorts, a privilege by no means common in my immediate circle of friends, some of whom thought me quite daring. In fact I was fifteen before I first wore trousers in public, and by then I had scratched my knees on a good many bramble bushes.

Walking-sticks, for young and old alike, were another standard piece of blackberry picking equipment. You used your stick to pull down the high branches which you would not otherwise be able to reach; you used it to push your way through where the growth was thick; and especially you used it to batter down any stinging nettles you might encounter. It was also useful if cows came too close for comfort; a sharp tap from your walking-stick would soon clear them out of the way. Indeed, it is not possible to pick blackberries properly without a walking-stick and I view with some horror the frequent spectacle of the modern holidaymaker, stick-less and wearing unsuitable sandals, picking what pass for blackberries along the verge of some dusty and polluted main road. The berries you picked at Tangies hardly needed to be washed; in an hour or so, if you did not stop too often and eat too many, you could fill a great gleaming basketful, sufficient for pie today and jam not merely for tomorrow, but right through the winter.

Just down the road from Tangies farmhouse was a ford, which in summer was very low indeed, and sometimes dried up to a mere trickle, but in winter became quite a torrent. A footbridge crossed this ford at the side of the road. It was here that I came to grief one Sunday morning in spring when, eager to gather the primroses which grew in masses on the bank beyond, I elected to walk through the ford instead of going round over the bridge. The water was not deep; it was the time of the spring drought. I was sure I would be safe. Unfortunately I took no account of the film of green algae which grew where the water ran over the concrete bed of the ford. In classic comedy fashion I found myself sitting in the water, drenched to the skin, and to make matters worse I was wearing my best skirt and jumper. The misery of that day remained with me for a long time.

Our friends at the farm had a daughter, named Joyce, who was four years older than me, and of heavier build. It was in Joyce's borrowed clothes that I trudged home across Loe Bar, my feet cold and clammy in my own damp boots. The congregation was just coming out of Peverell Road chapel as we passed the door, and I sensed a hundred pairs of eyes on the hemline of Joyce's gym-slip which, in spite of being hitched up round the waist, was flapping hopelessly round the lower part of my legs. I resolved to be much more careful where I stepped on future visits to Tangies: alas for my good resolutions; that same summer I fell head-first into a bed of stinging nettles, one of the most uncomfortable experiences of my life.

The farms grouped around the Loe Pool, of which Tangies is one, had lovely romantic names; Content, Pentire, Nanspean, Eglosderry, Killianker, Carminowe and Winnianton. These last two named were old manor houses, owned by the Penrose Estate, thus giving Captain Rogers at Penrose the impressive title of 'Lord of the Manors of Penrose, Carminowe and Winnianton'.

When I was about nine or ten years old, I began to hear whisperings among the grown-ups that certain farms were going to be 'taken'. Among these were Higher and Lower Content, Eglosderry (which I always imagined to be spelt Eggless Dairy and which puzzled me a great deal on this account) and Killianker. I was not sure for what purpose these farms were to be taken but I gathered that it was all very serious, for the adults spoke about it in the same hushed tones as they used when they told each other that people were dying. Once, I caught the word Admiralty and gradually it dawned upon my understanding that soon these lovely farms would be no more; the Admiralty were going to build something called a Naval Air Station on the land.

I had no idea what a Naval Air Station might be, but it sounded very ugly, and so, indeed, it proved to be. Many people welcomed it; certainly it brought work and great prosperity to Helston, Porthleven and the surrounding area. But hangars and runways are not beautiful things, and it is hard to have to see such ugliness displacing the green pastures you have known and loved all your life. They called it Culdrose after another of the farms which had to be taken. I was glad they did not call it Killianker. To take so lovely a word and to apply it to that vulgar rash of brick and concrete would surely have been an insult too great to be borne. So Killianker died, and Eglosderry died, and Content died, and as they buried them beneath Number One runway I began to be aware for the first time of a long-shadowed ogre named Progress, whose feet were destined in so short a time to stamp unnecessarily hard upon so many of the beautiful things to which I had grown accustomed, which had always been there and which, in the blind faith of childhood, I had foolishly supposed always would be.

CHAPTER 6

Lighted Windows

I had entered my twelfth year and was beginning to feel that I was very grown up. It was a time of great events and considerable change. The war in Europe ended, appropriately for us, on Flora Day, and the dancing in the streets of Helston took on a wild and carefree abandon. The girls in the children's dance wore red, white and blue ribbon in their hair that year, instead of the traditional flowers, and the streets were decked with Union Jacks. In the matter of flags, however, it would have been hard for Helston to out-do Porthleven, particularly Thomas Street, where it was difficult to walk up the pavement without becoming entangled in bunting and streamers. There was dancing in the streets that night and, wonder of wonders, lighted windows. People left their curtains drawn back, so you could see right into the rooms, which gave you a warm, glowing feeling, like being at innumerable parties all at once. Unable to properly remember any dark other than that intense, all-encircling dark of the blackout, I found it a thrilling experience to implement my dream of walking about the lighted streets and indeed, during the whole of the next winter Mabel and I would frequently walk around the village in the early evening, for no other purpose than that of revelling in the pleasure of

96

street-lighting, and the sheer delight of being out of doors after dark.

Just about the time of the VE celebrations I sat the exam which came to be known as the Eleven plus but which was then simply called the scholarship. I had been made aware of the existence of the scholarship at a very early stage in my school career, when an acquaintance of my mother, with whom we were having tea, exclaimed enthusiastically "I'll give you ten shillings if you pass the scholarship." I never forgot her promise though alas, she did, and I do not think that I shall receive the ten shillings now.

The day of the examination dawned cold and grey and gloomy as spring mornings sometimes are. It was Church School's turn to be the examination centre that year, and a little group of us trooped thither, very nervous, clutching pencil-cases and rulers, and terrified lest we should make fools of ourselves by going to the wrong place. In fact this was precisely what we did, and in consequence we had to troop forlornly through a classroom of older children to reach the exam room, conscious of their comments and titters as we passed by. The examination room itself was very small: the invigilators were two local worthies, a retired draper named Trevaskis, who had piercing blue eyes and a patriarchal shock of white hair, and a spinster lady called Miss Kenchington, who was a pillar of the Red Cross and who sometimes gave us folk-dancing lessons on her back lawn, aided by a gramophone and hindered by a rather unruly Pekingese dog. Neither the dog nor the gramophone was in evidence today: we would have preferred either to the ordeal we were about to face.

The desks were spaced as far apart as possible, which was not very far, since there were between fifteen and twenty candidates in the tiny room, and I was in an agony lest a casual glance in someone else's direction should be construed as an attempt to cheat, and disqualify me. I therefore kept my eyes glued to my work, only looking up occasionally towards the front, where Miss Kenchington was knitting something voluminous in knubbly orange wool, and Mr Trevaskis was gazing slowly around the room, swivelling his blue eyes from side to side very intently. The day seemed interminable. In the morning we did arithmetic and answered those peculiar questions which always begin 'Bill is three years older than Hazel but two years younger than John . . .' After lunch we wrote essays and coped with grammar and comprehension tests. Miss Kenchington's knitting grew to vast proportions and Mr Trevaskis' eyes swivelled in time with the slow, insistent ticking of the clock. Convinced that we had failed, but relieved that it was all over, we trooped home.

Some weeks later I found that I was amongst those who had not failed, and in the autumn of that same year I went to the Grammar School at Helston. Before this, however, the evacuees had gone home, the first atom-bomb had been dropped on Hiroshima, and the war was really over. It was very strange, watching the evacuees climb back into their coach to go to the station, five years older than when they had first come, most of them a good deal healthier and better dressed. They had come in tears and they went in tears. Edna Smiff wept copiously and promised to write, and to come down on holiday. In fact I have never seen or heard from her since. Many of them did come back: few summers pass without a strangely familiar face appearing in the village, and one gropes in the back of one's mind for a name, for another, younger edition of the same face, and a cockney accent of long ago. Pat Wogan, Vera Svedlitz, Helen Reiterbund, Maureen Buckley, June Ellis – one day they were there, and the next they were gone, and soon it was as if they had never been there at all. Some of them stayed, however. They had grown up in the village, had met and married local boys and girls. Their children were Porthleveners by birth, and spoke with Cornish voices. In many ways this injection of new blood was a good

98

thing. Had not Dr Elliston said, in one of his expansive moments, "Porthleveners are inter-bred, under-fed and a damn lot of lunatics"? The latter two of these three allegations may have been more fancy than fact on the doctor's part – certainly I have never seen much sign of malnutrition or mental disorder in the village, but it is undeniable that pre-war Porthleven was severely interbred and fiercely insular. The war, at least, had freed us from these chains.

Dr Elliston himself retired when the war was over. Choleric and outspoken, he had a reputation for frightening his patients into recovery. His surgery was a terrible old place in an outhouse adjoining his home. It had, at one time, been a stable, and still bore a strong resemblance to one, being unpainted and none too clean. Often there was straw from packing cases strewn on the floor, for the doctor had much of his dispensing done on the premises, and bottles of intriguing substances were delivered there and stored in the loft over the surgery. One story told of him is that he persistently prescribed a substance designated ADT for a certain local hypochondriac. The patient thrived on this, and recommended it to his friends, one of whom ventured to ask the doctor what the initials stood for. "Any damn thing," growled Dr Elliston, who never suffered fools gladly, though he acted the fool outrageously himself. If you were in bed with measles or mumps and he came to visit you, he would often arrive singing raucously, and would take advantage of your weakened position to give you a hearty slap on your bare stomach: this was his particular version of the bedside manner. It was whispered by the adults that he drank more than he should: but they tended to say this of so many people that you wondered if they really knew what they were talking about. Certainly if Dr Elliston drank to excess the money must have come from some source other than his practice, which must have been far from lucrative, due to his generosity where medical fees were concerned. Terrified though most of us were of him, we missed him dreadfully when he went. We were fortunate in that his successor Dr Reeves seemed to understand us very well, and fitted easily into the community in a very short time.

Other new faces began to appear on the scene. People from the Ministry of Works: all manners and kinds of surveyors and building contractors and administrators. Then the Navy arrived. The village grew. Council houses sprouted in huge estates round the outskirts of Porthleven and Helston. They called our first new street Gibson Way after the war hero, Guy Gibson, whose grandparents lived in Porthleven and who spent much of his childhood in the village. It is a little sad to reflect that Guy Gibson and those others whose names were added to the roll on the War Memorial would probably neither recognise nor particularly approve of the sort of place into which Porthleven has grown.

All this, however, was still far in the future as we hurled ourselves with enthusiasm into the VJ celebrations. At eleven, you are still young enough to enjoy things wholeheartedly. The self-inflicted boredom which is the curse of teenagers has not yet assailed your spirit; the nuances of sorrow which underlie every joy in adult life are not yet apparent. So we shrieked with pure pleasure when they burned Hitler's house in the middle of the harbour, and spared not a thought for the thousands whose homes had really been burned and who were homeless because of the war. We waved our flags and cheered our returning heroes, heedless, in those hours of joy, of those who would not return. Our faces lit up with delight when they let off fireworks from the pier – we could barely remember what fireworks looked like. Golden rain and silver showers and great bursts of red and green stars – it was Victory Night and everything was light and bright and beautiful. That legacy of darkness which the war had left behind it and which would cast its ugly shadows down the years of our century was something we could not possibly have understood; nor would the grown-ups have wished us to – not that night when joy was bursting out all over the village. We danced on the square to the music of accordions. My father taught me to waltz – and our friends applauded as we circled around, and laughed when we tripped over one of the jam jars which had been set up as candle-holders to augment the lighting. People sang and shouted and were drunk, but I cannot remember that anyone was offensive. We were growing up and it was going to be a wonderful, wonderful world.

Where does childhood end? When time has blurred the edges of your memory it is hard to say. You realise, on the one hand, that you were not the adult you thought you were at fourteen; on the other, that the fond concept you treasure of your innocence and purity at ten or eleven years old is probably no more than a figment of your imagination. Certainly by the time I went to school in Helston I had begun to be thrust out of the ideal world of a child's imaginings, into a reality where endings were not always happy; where people were hurt and suffered and sometimes died, and nobody could do anything about it. Before I was eleven I had attended two funerals. The concept of allowing children to be present at such functions seems to fill many modern parents and teachers with shocked horror: it is, it seems, a traumatic, damaging experience for a sensitive child to be subjected to the finality of death in this particular way. For myself, I can only say that I rather enjoyed the grandeur of it all, and felt not the slightest horror, even though the deceased in one instance was a boy of twelve who had been killed when he rode his bicycle too fast out of Mill Lane and shot under a bus. Horrified though we were by the fact of his death, it nonetheless lent dignity and style to our lives to be commanded to attend his funeral to represent the school. We watched the proceedings with fascination; stood when everyone else stood, and sat with bowed heads when they did. We squeezed out a tear or two when the flower-decked coffin was carried out of the chapel, but this did not hurt us; indeed, it was a lesson in compassion, as we tried to identify ourselves with the feelings of the mourners.

The other funeral we attended was a very splendid affair, the deceased having been a prominent member of the chapel and highly respected throughout the village. She had been responsible, amongst other things, for founding an organization called the Junior Guild, to which I belonged and it was felt appropriate that the Junior Guild should walk at the head of the procession and carry the flowers. We were highly elated at the honour, and dressed with care in navy-blue mackintoshes and berets. Unfortunately there was a downpour of rain, and the wet moss from the bases of the wreaths rubbed off on our fronts, leaving unsightly green stains, and into the bargain most of us were soaked to the skin and had wet feet, necessitating the heating of bath water at short notice; nevertheless I found the experience highly enjoyable, and regaled my parents over tea with descriptions of the various floral tributes and the messages appended to them. I felt no sense of shock or horror at all; merely understanding that people die just as they are born, and marry, and produce children. It was about this time that some of us discovered that this last-mentioned function could be performed by unmarried people, and the consequent scandalmongering in corners of the school playground knew no bounds for about a week, until some more interesting topic arose to take its place.

Our early days at the Grammar School were fearful and delightful. The building seemed inordinately large, and for a few days you kept getting lost. It was also bewilderingly modern; having been built in 1939, it was the newest building most of us had ever entered in our entire lives, and there was a strangeness about its light, airy style which, while pleasing, was at the same time a little awe-inspiring. Our first form room was the chemistry lab, which always smelled strongly of hard-boiled eggs, though whether this was from the genuine article, contained in people's packed lunches, or whether it was merely a strange by-product of the acids, one could not be sure.

Most people in our form preferred to bring packed lunches rather than eat school dinners, which were exceedingly revolting at that time. Those who brought their own food were known as the cold dinner people and I numbered amongst their ranks for a while, until I became brave enough to sample the official offering. On one occasion the cold dinner people began to eat their sandwiches before grace had been said in the hall, with the consequence that the mistress on duty that day rose to her feet and with a pained expression declaimed "For what *most* of us are *about* to receive, and for what *some* of us have *already* received, may we be made truly thankful." This oration seemed to me to be rather contrary to the spirit of the thing, but the teacher in question was not a highly successful disciplinarian, and I suppose she had to have some outlet for her feelings.

One of the highspots of the school day was the journey to and fro on the bus. We prided ourselves that ours was the rowdiest of all the school buses, and swelled with pleasure when the headmaster announced after prayers, as he frequently did "I have had complaints about the behaviour on the Porthleven bus." Violence was apt to break out at times, with caps, hats, books and satchels being flung about in what was nothing more than a turmoil of high spirits, but which some members of the public not unnaturally found offensive. The buses were dreadful old vehicles, either pre-war models or built to austerity specifications with wooden, slatted seats, and they rattled like cattle trucks on the way to market. One of our favourite diversions, particularly on the homeward journey, was to persuade the drivers to race. The volume of traffic on the road was never heavy at that time, and many of the drivers, young men recently released from the forces, were only too delighted to oblige us.

Our bus, a relief vehicle travelling to Porthleven only, would leave Helston station at about four o'clock, and was followed immediately by a through bus to Penzance, which followed the same route. The object of the exercise was to ensure that the bus in which you were travelling reached Porthleven square before the other. We became quite feverish in our excitement during these races, and resorted to the most dangerous devices in order to keep in the lead. Halfway between Helston and Porthleven there is a request stop known as Dry Tree. At Dry Tree a friend of mine, named Sylvia, and her two younger sisters who attended primary school in Helston, had to disembark to walk to the nearby farm where they lived. Precious time could be lost in this exercise, and on one or two occasions we were overtaken by the Penzance bus while we were stopped, with hoots and jeers all round. Subsequently, we devised a system whereby we did not actually stop at Dry Tree. The driver merely slowed the bus down to a crawl, and one of the senior boys, Gerald Richards, would pick up Sylvia and her sisters one by one and toss them out into the hedge. They had no objection whatever to this treatment, the smaller children shrieking with delight when their turn came; nevertheless we never tried this trick when the inspector was aboard.

The return of young men from the forces meant that we could have a football team again, and Saturday afternoons in the winter became devoted to this sport. Devotion was certainly needed, since you had to walk a distance of about two miles out of the village to the football pitch, which was laid out on Treza Downs. There was no shelter of any description for the spectators, and precious little for the players, who changed their clothes in a galvanized iron shack, and went home after the game mud-stained and unbathed. There was no nonsense about paid players, and every man in the team was a Porthleven man. We knew them all personally; they became our great new heroes, and we cheered them to victory on many a bitterly cold and wet day. In their first season they won a cup; two seasons later they won three, and the reputation of Porthleven as a footballing community was re-established. An under-eighteen team, named Pothleven Rovers, drew almost as much support as the first eleven, though our enthusiasm for these players was not uninfluenced by our purely physical interest in them as members of the opposite sex.

The Town Band, when it came back into being, was another unfailing source of interesting male material, though it was some time before the glamour of braided uniforms was added. The band in the early stages of its reformation was merely a handful of enthusiasts who tramped about the village on high days and holidays blowing such tunes as 'Standard of St George' on an assortment of elderly instruments; a far cry from the elegantly uniformed, well-rehearsed band of today. Yet I am convinced that I will never again be so moved by any music as I was by the sound of 'Oh come all ye faithful' when for the first time in my life I heard the lovely old Christmas melodies floating through a frosty winter night that was thick with stars, and thought that I had never heard anything so beautiful.

Christmas, in common with other annual festivals, suddenly seemed to be recurring with an almost alarming frequency and this, I was solemnly assured by my elders, was a sure sign of advancing age. I had reached that stage where most of my Christmas presents were entirely unsuitable; books, chosen by well-meaning relatives were usually hopelessly childish, and were read from cover to cover in about an hour: I no longer wanted toys, and the things I did want were at that time either too expensive, too sophisticated, or unobtainable owing to post-war austerity conditions. The American parcels, however, would usually yield up a couple of pairs of nylon stockings intended for my mother, but since she disliked nylons and never wore them, they were passed on to me. I paraded about in them to the envy of my friends and the detriment of my own natural modesty; I had always had good long legs and considered myself highly elegant in my transatlantic hose, which helped in some measure to compensate for my broken front tooth, (caused when I was pushed flat on my face in Board School playground during a particularly boisterous game of rounders) and for the fact that my hair obstinately refused to curl in the fashion of the time, even when I screwed it up in pipe cleaners on Saturday nights. Mabel managed to persuade her mother to let her have a perm, but my parents did not like the idea, and it was several years before the ministrations of the local hairdresser were permitted to attempt a dubious improvement upon the state of my straight locks.

Mabel also possessed a second-hand bicycle, which I rather coveted, but my father was none too keen on my having a bike of my own. I did nothing to further his confidence in me as a cyclist when I purloined his own machine one day and fell off it, knocking my head against a wall in the process and collapsing in an unconscious heap on the ground. So I never owned a bicycle, though Mabel was highly generous with hers, and we used to go up to Cemetery Lane, which was fairly flat and traffic-free, for me to learn to ride. I was doing very well, and could manage to ride to the Vicarage, turn round in the road and coast back to the cemetery gates without falling off, when one day we were overtaken by near disaster. Ronnie Benney owned a horse – a hunter of brutish disposition, which was continually getting out from whatever field it had been put into, and making a nuisance of itself. On this particular day it got out into Cemetery Lane when we were there with the bicycle. Certain that we should be kicked to death, we rushed inside the cemetery and peered, trembling, from

106

behind the tombstones, hoping that the sight of us would not cause him to leap the hedge in pursuit. Mabel was frantic for the safety of her bicycle, which we could not get through the turnstile-type gate of the cemetery and had to leave it outside in the hedge. She was sure it would be trampled to pieces. The day was saved, however, by the appearance of Ronnie Benney, brandishing a halter, and the recalcitrant horse was led home in disgrace yet again, while we emerged, white-faced and trembling, to collect an undamaged bicycle; but we never went cycling in Cemetery Lane again. In any event, we had begun to look for more sophisticated leisure pursuits.

It was at about this time that the Mobile Cinema came to Porthleven. The owner of this enterprise, who lived at Mullion, would hire one film per week and take it round all the villages in turn. Thursday nights was our turn, and half the village would pack itself into the Public Hall on these occasions. The seating was somewhat rudimentary, though after a while it became possible to hire a cushion at the door on payment of an extra threepence. In accordance with time-honoured custom, all the courting couples sat at the back, and the rowdies went to the front, in order to get as far away as possible from the projectionist, who nevertheless would sometimes have to stop the film and insist on quietness before proceeding. The rest of us sat in the middle of the hall, chewing sweets in the darkness and getting a vicarious thrill out of the effect of Margaret Lockwood's beauty on her leading man.

The Public Hall was in continual demand in the early post-war years for various events, one of the great annual ones being the musical festival, held in the autumn, and lasting two days. The Saturday night was particularly exhausting, and we would sit from six o'clock till about 11.30 listening to innumerable tenors warbling 'Silent Worship' and equally innumerable sopranos wavering through the Fairy Song from *The Immortal Hour*. We always liked the male duet class best, when you were bound to hear 'Excelsior', which in spite of its idiotic words was a rousing piece and made good listening.

The first summer after the war was over, they decided to hold a Gala Week to raise funds for a new recreation ground, and this was the beginning of what became for many years an annual occasion. In its heyday it was carried out with considerable splendour, and great arches of greenery were erected across the square, while banners reading 'Welcome to our Gala' were hung up everywhere. There were gymkhanas for horses and for motor cycles; a huge carnival and a torchlight procession which looked very picturesque, though usually the participants ended up covered in candle-grease. The biggest event of all was the Quayside Carolare which, alas, became too famous for its own good, and was copied by innumerable villages around West Cornwall, thus losing the element of novelty which gave it its impact. But it was a moving experience to be one of the many thousands who in those early days would gather round the harbour for the hymn-singing, even though for many the whole thing was more a tourist attraction than an act of worship.

Later in the summer, after Gala Week was over, the Town Band would hold Water Sports, and we would again foregather at the Harbour head to watch local swimmers compete against beefy types from Newlyn, who usually gave a display of water polo to end the proceedings. There were always a few tense moments at these sports when Squire Rogers, who was the band's president, and who always insisted on acting as starter for the races, was got on and off the committee boat, he being extremely elderly and suffering from stiffness following a badly fractured leg. Everyone would be terrified lest he fell into the water, but he had considerable confidence in himself, and never did.

When I was thirteen I learned to swim myself at long last. Most Porthleven children of my generation could swim by the time they were seven or eight; some rather earlier, but I was naturally timid of the water, and Porthleven beach, with its vicious undertow and its 'truck' – a drop of nearly two feet deep just beyond low tideline, – was not a very suitable place for a nervous learner to master the art of swimming. Even when I could swim I always hated it, and really only went to the beach because everyone else did. Sometimes we swam in the harbour, which I found even more frightening, with its slippery rocks and deep, murky green water. I was always clumsy in water. For instance, other people seemed to be able to take a rest, when swimming in the harbour, by hanging on casually to the side of a punt: when I did so, my legs got sucked underneath the punt and I could only push myself away again with extreme difficulty. On one famous occasion we were swimming in the outer harbour at high tide and I was dared by Rosa's sister Shirley to jump off the quay. I hesitated: I had never attempted this feat, though most of the boys and one or two of the better swimmers amongst the girls did it regularly. Shirley, although she was a bit of a dare-devil, had never done it either. She promised that if I would jump first, she would follow. I might never have made the jump if I had not spied a certain boy swimming in the middle of the harbour. He was a holidaymaker; one of the regulars who came every year to Porthleven, and we thought he was marvellous because he went to a minor public school and spoke with the corresponding accent. He was also an extremely strong swimmer, far more stylish than most of the local boys. Might he not be impressed if I were to jump off the quay? Vanity overcame fear, and I jumped.

If I close my eyes I can still see the rush of white spray and the darkness – that terrible green darkness – closing in on me, folding itself about me . . . pushing me down and down and down . . . I opened my mouth to scream . . . Suddenly there was sunlight again, and a blur of faces, and the sound of laughter, mingling with the sorry sound of my awful gasps for breath. Half faint from fright and feeling very sick because of the quantity of filthy harbour water I had swallowed, I managed to swim the few yards to the ladder and climb up onto the quay. The boy swam nearby with slow, disdainful strokes, hardly knowing whether to be amused or pained at my performance. Shirley stood on the quay, and announced that she had decided not to jump today after all. She never did, to my knowledge – and I never did again. I had suffered grievous loss of dignity, and the paltry achievement of jumping into the harbour at high tide was scarcely worth so great a sacrifice.

Swimming apart, however, my sporting abilities seemed to have improved over the years. I gained third place in the junior high jump at school, a feat attributable in no small measure to hours of practice in The Gue where, in heavy shoes and without any safety precautions whatever, we would leap over Michael Rosewarne's home-made high-jump stand, set up outside Ching's granite works where the road was flat enough to minimise the risk of falling and breaking one's ankle. The school field, with a mat to land on, seemed easy and luxurious by contrast. I also owed my place in the school second hockey eleven to my sporting activities in The Gue, where I had often kept goal for the boys when they were short of football players, and my experience in hard kicking stood me in good stead when I was appointed goalkeeper to the school team. Disaster struck, however, before I had even played in a match. The fixture was an away one against Truro High School, to be played on a Saturday afternoon, and I therefore took all my gear home with me on the Friday evening in readiness, placing it lovingly and proudly in my bedroom. Hurrying out the next day with my precious burden, my foot slipped on the top stair. I tried to steady myself but failed. I became tangled up in the gear, and remember nothing more until I came to my senses at the bottom of the stairs, where I found myself lying in

110

a coal scuttle with my head facing the front door and my feet pointing back up the stairs, having somersaulted as I fell. Somehow or other I was still clutching my hockey stick and leg-guards – and somehow or other I managed to totter to the square, catch the bus to Helston and join the rest of the team in the coach. Perhaps not surprisingly, we lost the match, though the two-nil result was hardly a disgrace in my rather concussed circumstances. I was the hero of the hour, and really rather enjoyed myself.

I never distinguished myself as a hockey player, and as time went on became increasingly disillusioned with my dangerous Aunt Sally rôle in the muddy goal mouth. I found that I was able to put my exhibitionist tendencies to better use on the stage. I had a fair talent for acting, and appeared in nearly all the school plays. These were seldom staged without incident, perhaps the most notable of which occurred when the Junior Girls presented a pageant of stories from the Asgard saga at the end of one summer term.

I had been cast as Baldur the Beautiful – a rôle which pleased me immensely, particularly since several much better-looking candidates had auditioned for the part. I was also well-pleased with my costume, which included a dashing cloak and a short, swirling, kilt-like affair in gold satin, which swung beautifully as I walked. Unhappily, however, the wardrobe mistress had been rather careless when making this garment, and the piece of elastic which supported the kilt at the waist snapped during performance. Fortunately I felt it go, and was in time to grasp it and prevent it from falling down, but for the duration of the play I was unable to move my arms because I was using both of them to hold up my skirt. Blind Hodur added to the general pandemonium when he missed me by feet with his mistletoe arrow, but I sank to the floor of the stage, still clutching my waistline, and died gracefully to the accompaniment of hilarious laughter and tumultuous, if ironic, applause.

The ill-starred Baldur was in fact the only 'pretty' part I ever managed to secure for myself in a school play. Having shown some aptitude in the rôle of an old woman, I was relentlessly cast as old women for the rest of my school career: this riled me, since I was apt to regard it more as an insult to my appearance than a compliment to my ability. In secret, I wrote plays with glamorous, romantic parts for myself, which I performed for my own entertainment in my bedroom and never dared to show anyone, lest I again became an object of ridicule. I did pluck up sufficient courage to submit one or two poems for the school magazine, and was greatly stimulated by seeing them in print. I had always written poetry, a fact which designated me eccentric, and oddly enough I never minded this label. Occasionally I was asked to recite in a concert, and encouraged by my mother, I began to recite my own poems on these occasions, which proved very popular, and I found myself performing in a variety of auditoriums, mainly village halls and Methodist schoolrooms, in places as far apart as Twelveheads near Truro, and St Just, beyond Penzance in the west.

These rather rustic occasions nevertheless contributed to my small stock of social poise, since they often necessitated my being entertained to tea or supper at the house of someone I had never met before, and as it was impracticable to maintain silence in these circumstances I began to try to master the art of making polite conversation with strangers, many of whom became friends in the fullness of time. Some of the hostesses, nonetheless, had rather weird ideas on how a young teenage guest should be entertained. You might find yourself shut, alone, in an unheated front parlour for about an hour before the performance ''so that you can rest up a bit.'' Or, on asking to go to the toilet, you might be ceremoniously conducted to a spare bedroom and offered a chamber-pot ''because 'tis awful muddy down across the yard . . .'' Perhaps worst of all, you might find yourself served with pink blancmange, or custard with the skin left on, or with lumps in it, and good manners demanded that you ate what was put in front of you, particularly in those austerity times. For the most part, however, you were well-fed, and well-received, and if, as sometimes happened, you got an encore at the end of your performance you went home feeling ten feet tall, and of star status.

It is usually hard to remember the last time you do anything. So often the occasion passes without your noticing – there is no realisation that it is, indeed, the last time and in the nature of things you are spared the poignancy which would have attended your understanding. So I cannot remember the last time my father carried me upstairs to bed, or the last time my mother read me a bedtime story. I cannot remember the last time I played Moppy or Woody or marbles or the last time I rode the broad, comfortable back of dear old Blossom. I cannot remember the last time the gang met in Paddy's Yard, sprawling in the summer weeds and inhaling the scent of the camomile that the weight of our bodies had crushed. If I could remember, then that remembrance would make me sad. As it is, I look back only on the warm pleasure of it all: for the pains of childhood are ephemeral and soon gone, leaving behind them only the best and happiest of memories.

For me, those memories are easier to touch than perhaps they are for some of my contemporaries. I am one of the deep-rooted people: I still walk those same streets; I still pass those same places where my childhood had its existence. Porthleven has changed, keeping some sort of pace with a changing, congested, urbanised world. The bungaloid development has come upon us. Fields – acres and acres of fields – are covered with buildings; neat, comfortable, rather soulless buildings. The children who live in them take for granted such conveniences as baths, with hot water on tap, and a fitted carpet on the sitting-room floor. They go to schools so well provided with modern equipment that the Helston Grammar School I knew would be an archaic sort of joke to them. But they can never have a dog show in the field behind the Vicarage, because now there is no field behind the Vicarage: indeed, the Vicarage itself has been sold, and a new one purchased in a different location. They will never pick primroses in Mill Lane, because the hedge that bore them was bulldozed down to make way for Methleigh Parc and Mill Close. They will never jump rivers in Dicky Wigs moors, and they will probably never see a steamer come into Porthleven harbour again. Maybe it doesn't matter. Maybe the Porthleven I knew and loved was not so lovely either.

Maybe it is a thing of no importance that the twin grocery shops which used to be Addie's and Gladys's have been knocked into one bald, uninteresting whole with an unadorned concrete front, and are used as a launderette. Maybe it is even a good thing that Willziz has been turned into a smart restaurant, and that the successors in title to Blight operate a bright little supermarket in new premises where Simons' shoe shop used to be. Maybe these things matter to no one except me – and only to me because I am excessively nostalgic and sentimental. Yet I cannot help being glad, as I look around the place, that I remember a Porthleven which to me was more real, more whole, more a genuine community than the Porthleven we have today. Its echoes remain: sometimes on a quiet day there can be a moment – engendered, perhaps by something as simple as a child with a dog, or the distant sound of a seagull – when I still seem to catch a glimpse of that other Porthleven; that warm-hearted soul-lifting, irritating, fascinating, wonderful Porthleven I used to know, just as sometimes, in the person time has forced me to become, I can sometimes hear the faraway echo of the little girl I used to be.

APPENDIX

SOME PORTHLEVEN NICKNAMES, PAST AND PRESENT

Arthur Corner
Annie Corner
Aw Caw
Any Bucket
Alker
Any Liver
Aint I Pretty
Annie Punctual
Annie Faa

Blue Light Buckle
Black Rough Bristol
Billy Bass Billy German
Bob Sturgeon (Bob Stuart) Battle Bah
Ben Turtle Bubby Sam
Baggy Belus
Bruno Barney
Buster Bottley
Bummer Bill Muller
Babe Buckshee
Bouncer Box Tail
Barnet Barber John
Bunker Bobby Bingo
Beffy Bracey
Bill Shee Black Beetle
Boxer Billy Raker
Burn-your-weed (Good Day) Brisha M'Cew (Bridget M'Cew)
Baby Bill Gogger
Big Letch Boll
Boss Bunghole
Buller Blazer
Bread-and-Butter-Guts Bumshee

Billy Squat Bowie
Buddy Billie Hardo
Butty Black Sal
Bob Billio Bessie Sovereigns
Bob Jail Bo
Bob Kick

Crab Electric (Edward Bex)(Massa)
Cush Ebbo
Chicken Ernie Malt
Charlie Hoss Eggy
Calcutta Erdy
Cane Ebby
Curly Edgar Dodus
Chug
Chum
Cap'n Stee Fuzzy
Crimea Figgy
Craylo Flamer
Cute Freddie Pudd'n
Coconut Fatty
Circulation (Joe Circ) Fishy
Cap'n Matt Fitcher
Crom Fatty Arbuckle
Clarinet Funny
Canugger Ferd
Crowdie Farewell
Crow Frankie Crab Pot
Cleent (Snow White) Frankie Pots
    Frog

Dillum Fat John
Dickie-Bo
Dick Bones
Dowshie Ginger Rough
Dicky Dart Green
Dumb Dicky Glacso Baby (Rice Pudding)
Ducky Gully
Dog Rough Georgie Nougat
Dunkirk Georgie Lad
Diddy Gains
Dicky Trad Gibbett
Dumps Gant
Dinks Googey
Dingle Great George
Daddy Guinea Pig
Dick Bubs Gaffer
Dick's William Gummy (Jan-be-beggared)
Drawf Gazer
Daily Mail Georgie Porgie
Didymus Good Day (Burn-your-weed)
Daisy

Dan Bawden
Dickie Sam

Hookey Joe Circ (Circulation)
Harry Hedgehog Joe Duck
Harvey Darvey Jack Right
Hummy Johnny Guy
Hannibal (Tucky) John Faddy
Henry Shilling Jessie
Henry-any-colour Jan-be-beggared (Gummy)
Helbie John Dinks
Haud-for-Haud Jimmy Duzzy
Homic Jim Al
Hucky Jack Shyte
   Jimmy Laura

Idly Do Jim Braddy
 Jo King

Jannard Joe Snobrag
Johnny Cats Jinny-fur
Jumbo Joe Rufus
Jeff Jenny Bird
Janie (The Big Splash)
Joe Beef Kipper
John Rooda Kneebone
Jaba Kifer
Joe Gook Keb
John Bean Kiss Watch Key (Keswatchkey)
Jimmy Squat King Curnow
Jim Bice Katie Pickles
Johnny Flea
Johnny Rabbit Lapwing
John Stag Liver
John the Gardener Long Peter (Tall Peter)
Jimmy the Gardener Long Dick
Jimmy Dowsey Leslie Boo
Johnny Lick (Leek?) Little Letch
Jack Sailor Landlord
Jellyfurt Licky Spoon
Johnny Ginger Lofty
Jack Goggy Legger
Jan Ivy Long Ned
Jack False Little Bob
Jock Lazarus
Jimmy Wha Limpet
Joppa Little Faa
Jack Gonger Lammo
   Little Acre
   Luss

Louie Dart
Lizzie Tipperary Peter Mullett
Liza Bingey Pluckybird
Lady Ben Packa
Lizzie Dur Poor Apple
Lizzie Figgy Popeye
Lollie Perks
Little Fay Priddo
Louie Tea Polish
Lily Pea Pard
    Par

Mem Porky
Matthe' Majort Porty
Massa (Electric)(Bex) Professor
Moo Perry
Mock Ivy Pincher
Mabjer Platty Foot
Mungey Pin
Mush Poochie
Master Paddy
Mastum Pilchard Dick
Marbeele Poker
Mash Piper
May Tosh Peter Feet
Miss Hush Peanut
    Petrol

Neddy Wicks Popsey
Niffer Peter Buddy
Nicky Nick Phyllis Dick
Nackers Priest
Ned Bush
Nugger Quaker
Nobby Quim
Ninnow
Ninnet Rice Pudd'n (Glacso Baby)
Nin Nin Rose Tree
Nuss Rusty
News-of-the-World Reds
    Rat

Osweth Rumpy Robbie Doubt
Oh Boy (Skitter) Rufus Rumpump
Owshwed Rougheart
    Rooster

Spitwinker Tatie Pie
Shaftoe Tushy
Stamen Tar Pot
Skwimp Taxi

118

Sudden The Big Splash (Janie)
Snares Tommy Alk
Skebs Tommy Chip
Scrollers (Oysters) Titch
Snowball Tall Peter (Long Peter)
Short Ned Trunk
Squinion Tommy Treacle
Scoop Tadpole
Stumpy Tough
Stubbitt Tommy Tittlemouse
Swepney Tal
Spider Tit-the-door
Scottie Tailey
Shinus Tiddley-Fino
Spain Twisty
Slabbie Tarzan
Sammer Tick Tick
Scholar Tommy Cuddle
Smitter (Oh Boy!) Tommy Hog
Spaley Turdy
Swifty Tommy-me-Friend
Swede Tom Pup
Sam Carleen Tom Sweet
Smith Turtle
Scout Tucky (Hannibal)
Sunny Jim Tullo
Swivel Tommy Tea
Sammy Dangey Tom Any
Swenny Tom Bex
Sippie Thunder
Snappers Tommy Mucky
Squirleys Tibby
Shimmy Tom Bucket
Swede Tom Gun
Sabu Tom Ar
Sunny Balls Tom Tifoot
Snow White Tommy Bonus
Swingarm Tiddley Mush
    Tom Donkeyman

Uncle John Tommy Cook
Uncle Tanner Thomas Fuggy
    Tammy

Willie-Bo
Wiggie
Wigs
Wops
Wrinkle
Willie Oysters (Scrollers)
Whale
Wesy Webb

119

Whiskey
Wesley
Workish
Willie Wiggie
Willie Bill
Willie Ivy
Wearne Ivy
Woozey

Some people had two, or even as many as three nicknames, and where I know this is the case, I have cross-indexed them on the list.